Change Matters

Making a difference in education and training

Geoff Scott

ALLEN & UNWIN

First published in 1999 by
Allen & Unwin
9 Atchison Street
St Leonards NSW 1590
Australia
Phone: (61 2) 8425 0100
Fax: (61 2) 9906 2218
E-mail: frontdesk@allen-unwin.com.au
Web: http://www.allen-unwin.com.au

National Library of Australia
Cataloguing-in-Publication entry:

Scott, Geoff, 1945– .
Change matters: making a difference in education and training.

Bibliography.
Includes index.
ISBN 1 86448 916 2.

1. Organizational change—Management. 2. School management and organization. I. Title.

658.406

Set in 11.5/13 pt Bembo by DOCUPRO, Sydney
Printed by SRM Production Services Sdn Bhd, Malaysia

10 9 8 7 6 5 4 3 2 1

CONTENTS

TABLES AND FIGURES

Tables

Figures

ACKNOWLEDGMENTS

This book is the product of twenty years' research on the change process in education. My original interest in the area was sparked by my friend and colleague Michael Fullan in the mid-1970s. The theory of change that underpins the book has emerged from joint work and a doctoral thesis undertaken with Michael, from my own work on innovations and change consultancies in technical, further and higher education and from the input of the hundreds of students at the University of Technology, Sydney who have undertaken courses on the subject over that time.

INTRODUCTION

*. . . good ideas with no ideas on how to put
them into practice are wasted ideas.*
Michael Fullan (1982)

Whereas many books on education address the 'what' of change this one addresses the 'how'.

It has been produced for the following reasons:

First, change is all around us. The need for both individuals and organisations to engage in continuous adaptation, enhancement and innovation is ongoing. Yet such processes are typically very poorly managed. There is more failure in change projects, even ones that everyone sees as necessary, than there is success. There is much talk about what must change in education, but when people get to work to put these desired developments into practice they often find themselves quite unsure of how best to proceed.

Second, the pressures for change are increasing, not decreasing. In a context in which education is coming under increasing scrutiny, in which it is facing significant cuts, in which technological change is increasing, and in which there are heightened levels of local and overseas competition we cannot rest on our laurels. In many instances a capability to manage change quickly and effectively is becoming essential to the survival of educational organisations and the jobs of the people who populate them.

Third, failed change costs. It costs economically but it also costs psychologically. When enthusiastic teachers, trainers, lecturers or educational managers commit to a change project and that project fails, they carry the scars of that experience with them. Students and the country receive no benefit from failed change. Individuals and organisations that take on a change project which fails suffer a loss of reputation and, particularly in the current economic climate, this may cost jobs.

Fourth, books on change have become increasingly popular in recent years. It is reported that some 800 were published in the US alone in the first half of the 1990s.[1] However, many of these are peddling 'change management snake oil'. What they advocate rests on very flimsy research foundations indeed. Some offer magic formulas which, when followed, achieve little. Others describe the change process but offer little by way of practical advice. In general there is a need to identify and question the change management myths which are being currently put about in education.

Fifth, much of the writing about change management comes from people working in industry and commerce and from academics in the area of business management. Such sources certainly have something to offer the educator. However, because their advice is not derived from an understanding of the unique operating context of education and training, it often misses the mark. What is needed, therefore, is an understanding of change and how to manage it which is located in the world of education rather than business. Such research is now available. Michael Fullan and Andy Hargreaves, from the University of Toronto, Canada, have done much to identify, undertake and disseminate change research in schools. However, much less has been achieved in this regard with educators operating in post-secondary education contexts such as training, community education and higher education or in early childhood education.

Sixth, there is a need to help educators 'see the forest for the trees', that is to identify, label and explore the links between all the components that make up the change management puzzle. For example, it is important to become clear on how the processes of individual and organisational change are linked, how change is a complex learning and unlearning process rather than an event and how, at the heart of change, are people, their values, beliefs, motives and relationships.

Finally, professional capability studies[2] repeatedly identify the ability to manage change as a core competency for effective professional performance. These studies also repeatedly emphasise that its development should be given a central place in educational programs at all levels.

What follows has been developed specifically to address the above needs. The material contained in this book was developed using a framework identified jointly by myself and Michael Fullan at the University of Toronto, Canada. Over the past twenty years this framework has been tested and refined during a wide range of the author's change consultancies within and beyond Australia and through workplace research undertaken by the many practising educators involved in the author's courses on managing change at the University of Technology, Sydney. What is brought together in the following chapters is, therefore, the distillation of the practical experience and critical inquiry of literally hundreds of teachers, lecturers, trainers and educational managers who, like all of us, have had to come to grips with the practicalities of continuous change.

The aim is to assist practising educators in all sectors and roles not only to develop their competence in managing their own change projects but also to contribute to the capability of the organisation in which they work to manage its overall improvement and innovation activities. Furthermore, it is intended to enable them to do so more rapidly than simply relying on their own resources and a process of trial and error.

Each of the six chapters which make up this book addresses an important component of what is necessary for efficient and effective change management in education and training. The book is organised so that learning from it can be a cumulative process. That is, the content covered in early chapters will directly assist in the understanding of later ones.

In Chapter 1, the dynamics of the change process in education are explored through the study of a range of change management analogies. The key factors that make up the process of change and their interconnection are identified. The central role which motivation, values, evaluation and micropolitics play in this process is discussed and an overall change management framework which takes account of these factors is then outlined. It is around this framework that the book is organised.

Chapter 2 offers a detailed investigation of the most effective way to manage the process of learning program innovation and enhancement. A comprehensive overview of the key components that make up a learning program is given, important quality tests are identified and the cyclical (as distinct from linear) nature of the program change process is highlighted. Detailed practical advice, based on successful program change studies, is given for the initiation, development, implementation, evaluation and continuation of learning program innovations and enhancements.

In Chapter 3, the focus shifts to the workplace milieu in which program innovations must be located. It stresses that there is little to be gained by individuals becoming more effective at program innovation and enhancement if the workplace in which such change projects are attempted is unsupportive. Approaches to quality assurance, improvement and innovation uniquely suited to education are identified and the key attributes of a workplace capable of continuous improvement and innovation are outlined. The aspects covered include workplace culture and climate, staff selection and support, ways of linking educational and administrative enhancements, constructive approaches to communication, decision making and structure.

In Chapter 4 an essential tool for undertaking continuous quality improvement and innovation in education—workplace action research—is examined. The place of this approach within the broader range of research methods available to educators is noted, its history briefly outlined, practical ways of using it illustrated and practice in its use given.

In Chapter 5 the implications for the individual as a manager of continuous improvement and innovation in education are identified with reference to the broad base of research now available on leadership and change. A framework for under-standing leadership capability derived from the study of effective educational leaders is discussed. The fact that everyone can be a leader of change in their own role and area of expertise is noted.

Chapter 6 highlights the need to look outwards and forwards. Useful ways of linking into broader networks are outlined, some potential futures for education presented and the implications for effective change management drawn. The chapter emphasises the important distinction between 'change' and 'progress'.

KEY TERMS

It is important that some key terms are defined at the outset and that a shared understanding of their meaning is developed. Many of these terms are regularly used when educational changes are being discussed. However, it has repeatedly been discovered that people often use them with quite different meanings in mind. This leads to considerable miscommunica-tion which typically results in disaffection and frustration.

Below is a selection of the terms commonly used when educational changes are considered. In reading them through, compare your definitions with those in the Glossary (p. 200). Undertaking such an exercise is a good initial way to get a feel for the content of what is to follow:

Capability	Impact	Motivation
Change	Implementation	Paradox
Change management	Innovation	Progress
Climate	Institutionalisation	Quality assurance
Community education	Knowledge	Quality control
Competence	Learning	Quality improvement
Contingent	Learning objective	Research
Culture	Learning organisation	Skill
Dissemination	Learning program	Stance
Education	Manage	Training
Enhancement	Micropolitics	Values
Evaluation	Milieu	Way of thinking
Higher order competencies		

LEARNING PRINCIPLES WHICH UNDERPIN THE BOOK'S CONSTRUCTION

It is becoming increasingly clear what sorts of learning tactics adults find most helpful. The book aims to adopt these.

For example, it is based on a 'two-way' view of learning in which theory and practice are directly linked whenever possible. This approach involves readers in investigating how well their personal experience matches up with a broader framework of good practice derived from research. One way this is achieved is to invite readers to undertake a series of reflective exercises. Another way is to encourage them to figure how to apply what is being advocated to their own specific educational changes and context. The book aims to help readers 'see the forest for the trees'—that is, it provides an overall framework which shows how *all* of the complex ingredients that make up the change process in education fit together. This can be used by readers to label what change tactics they are already handling well, to see more clearly where these fit into the bigger picture of change management and to identify aspects of their current practice which need enhancement.

Finally, the book is constructed specifically to develop readers' confidence and skills in directing their own learning. This ability is vital in a period of such constant and rapid change, a period in which educators have to continuously improve and update their skills and knowledge. In this regard, Chapter 4 (Workplace research for continuous improvement and innovation) and Chapter 5 (The effective leader of change) should be particularly helpful.

In summary, the book seeks to facilitate direct links, whenever possible, between personal learning and what we know about effective program and workplace change.

REFLECTIVE EXERCISES

As noted above, the book incorporates a series of reflective exercises. These can be undertaken individually or with colleagues. They are included at key moments throughout the book where an understanding of what is being proposed will be enhanced by active reflection on the part of the reader.

The reflective exercises used come in a variety of forms. Some involve readers in comparing a case study with their own change experiences, using the good practice frameworks contained in the book. Some invite reflection on past experience. Others encourage readers to explore how best to apply what is being advocated to change projects in which they are currently involved. In the final chapter of the book a hypothetical is also included.

Those reflective exercises which focus on case study analysis involve a fictionalised version of material drawn from the author's experience with actual change projects. They have been carefully selected to reflect the wide range of operating contexts of educators—from school education through to adult community education, training in industry and higher education.

1

HOW THE CHANGE PROCESS IN EDUCATION WORKS

You can't be too far ahead of the march of progress. Wait until you hear the music coming up the corridor and open the door just before it arrives.

J.K. Galbraith

In this chapter you will be asked to reflect on your past experiences with educational change and from this to identify your views on how it works. You will then be invited to compare your conclusions with a summary of research on change dynamics. In doing this, a number of popular change management myths will be exposed.

In this chapter an overview of the key factors that usually trigger a change effort and influence the way it turns out is also given. Key sources of educational change are identified, the main types of change are noted, the way in which the scope and size of the change play a part is illustrated, and the central roles played by motivation, values and evaluation are outlined. These are brought together into an overall picture of how the change process in education operates. It is this conceptual framework[1] that underpins the whole book. In subsequent chapters each component of the framework is explored in detail.

In this chapter you are also given an opportunity to practise using the framework by seeing if it helps you make sense of a change management case study.

THE DYNAMICS OF CHANGE: EDUCATORS' CHANGE ANALOGIES

One of the most useful ways to develop a quick, overall feel for what practitioners' day-to-day experiences of change in education and training entail is to invent a personal analogy which describes them.[2]

Consider the analogies in the following list. They are some of the more common ones developed by practitioners in a wide range of teaching and management roles in education over the years.[3]

Educators' Change Analogies

When I am involved in change I feel like I am a:

- guide;
- coach;
- director of a play;
- chef in a restaurant;
- potter;
- surfboard rider on the waves of change;
- person negotiating a swamp;
- skipper on an ocean-going yacht;
- World War II general;
- person having a baby;
- swimmer in a tidal pool;
- mechanic trying to fix a car while it is going 100 kph;
- whitewater rafter;
- father confessor;
- juggler balancing spinning plates on the end of sticks;
- person in an Escher drawing.

The analogies in the above group were given by educational managers; those which follow were given by teachers and trainers:

- crew member;
- member of a chorus line;
- fellow traveller;
- person learning to cook for themselves;
- collector;
- creature in metamorphosis;
- piece of clay being moulded;
- person all at sea;
- bouncing ball;
- person on an icy slide;
- person going up a down escalator.

Now consider the following questions:

1 What, in general terms, are these analogies telling us about the nature of the change process in education?
2 How and why do these analogies vary?
3 Either select the analogy from the list that best matches your current experience of the change process in education or make up a new one.
   a Briefly write down how your selected analogy works and why it best describes your experience. For example, what does it say about the nature of the change process for someone in your position?
   b How might your role (for example, as teacher, administrator, manager etc.) and the amount of experience you have had in that job influence the sort of analogy chosen?
4 Compare and contrast your results with the summary of research on the nature of the change process in education in the following section.

Research on the dynamics of change

The change analogies presented above point to many of the key findings from research on the nature of the change process in education (Fullan, 1991, 1993; Scott, 1990, 1996c). They reveal, for example, that the change process:

Is uncertain

Things never go completely as predicted. There will always be that unexpected twist or surprise. No educational change, whether it be a program innovation or a workplace improvement, ever unfolds exactly as planned. The greater the scope and degree of change the greater the uncertainty.

Operates in phases

There is a time when a need for change is identified, a time when people start work on figuring out how best to handle it, a time when they start to implement their plan and a time when they seek to consolidate their change.

Is cyclical not linear

Although the change process does involve different phases, it is wrong to assume that these unfold in a 'one-off', linear fashion. No educational change is ever fixed or permanent. The local and external context in which education takes place is too volatile. Because of this the change process is best seen as operating in a cyclical fashion. This means that, with each innovation, it will be necessary to proceed through the various phases of change many times as the context in which the innovation operates alters. Some changes remain relevant for years and require only ongoing enhancement, others may have to be dropped because they cease to be feasible or relevant.

Is composed of a mix of factors beyond and within one's control

Any change effort always involves a mix of factors: those beyond the individual's control (for example, in the yacht analogy, the ocean) and those within one's influence (for example, how much sail to carry or what course to chart). This proposition: 'Denies that we are merely determined as products of our history and development; it also denies that we are entirely free to produce the world and history we desire regardless of the historical circumstances in which we find ourselves' (Kemmis, in Boud, 1985: 148).

As the educators' change analogies reveal, the degree of authority and responsibility inherent in the role of individuals affects the extent to which they can actively influence how things turn out or are at the mercy of outside forces. Consider, for example, the difference in this regard between the play director and the bouncing ball analogies.

Is reciprocal

What happens at one point in time will influence how things turn out at a later point. For example, if individuals have a negative experience early on in a change project this helps shape their reactions to it later on. The change process is reciprocal in another way—each new change effort both influences and is influenced by the milieu in which it is attempted. As Parlett and Dearden (1977: 15) found in their studies of change in higher education in the 1970s, 'The introduction of an innovation sets off a chain of repercussions throughout the learning milieu. In turn, these unintended consequences are likely to affect the innovation itself, changing its form and moderating its impact.'

Requires educators who can 'read and match'

Given the complex number of factors involved in any change effort and the fact that each of these factors is itself constantly shifting, what any individual does will always depend on being able to 'read' what is going on in each unique situation and 'match' the most appropriate response.[4] That is, what is done must always be contingent[5] on what the unique circumstances of each case dictate is feasible, appropriate and desirable. No decision in educational change management is, therefore, context free. For example, in the surfing analogy above, how one rides the waves of change will always depend on the size of the waves, their breaking characteristics on the day, the number of other surfers in the water and their relative position, the prevailing wind and so on. Of course, the greater the surfer's experience the more accurate the reading and the more skilled the response.

5

Change management myths

If one reviews the plethora of change management books now on the market[6] and the advice being given by many of the change gurus who now abound, much of what they advocate fails to take account of the context and dynamics outlined above. A number of myths keep cropping up.[7] They include:

- *The knight on a white charger myth* All that is necessary is to appoint a dynamic, reform-oriented leader and successful change is assured.
- *The consensual myth* A proposed change will only work if everyone it affects has approved of it; that is, a 'bottom up' approach to change always works.
- *The linear myth* Change proceeds in a fixed, one-off, linear fashion from initiation through development, implementation and institutionalisation.
- *The brute logic myth* Change is achieved by brute logic; that is, provided the proponent's argument for a change is compelling, those it affects will automatically adopt it.
- *The change event myth* Change is an event, like the launch of a new policy or curriculum rather than being a long iterative learning (and unlearning) process for all its participants.
- *The silver bullet myth* There is a set procedure which, if followed, will guarantee successful change.
- *The one size fits all myth* All that is necessary is to develop a standardised, 'teacher proof' curriculum or procedure and users will implement it fully and exactly as intended in every location across the system.
- *The either/or myth* Change management involves having to make rigid choices between, for example, taking a 'top-down' or a 'bottom-up' approach, giving clear direction or allowing a large degree of flexibility, adopting an organisation wide or a local emphasis, focusing on enhancement or innovation.

THE KEY INGREDIENTS IN THE EDUCATIONAL CHANGE PROCESS

The change process is complex because so many factors may be simultaneously interacting. It is important to develop an overview of these in order to reduce the feeling that one is always going to be a victim of mysterious forces. Labelling these factors and understanding the many ways in which they interact helps provide a starting point for effective change management in education. What emerges provides a series of checkpoints which can be used to make sure a potentially relevant influence has not been overlooked as the change process unfolds.

A wide range of sources and influences

Each change situation is shaped by a unique mix of external, system and local factors. In some cases external or even system factors have far less influence than local ones, for example, the teacher who decides to introduce a new learning resource into an existing class. In others, external and system factors are far more significant, for example, a system-wide introduction of computer-assisted learning. External influences such as changes in technology, the economy, work or social values can, through government policy and funding guidelines, play an important role in shaping the overall change agenda for education. System influences, for instance the structure and decision-making process of a large education department, can also either help or hinder the management of continuous innovation and enhancement. At the local level, the culture, climate and quality of leadership in the workplace, along with the nature and expectations of the student body, the standard of equipment and available facilities, will also play a part.

Table 1.1 summarises some of the major conditions, procedures and individuals that can trigger an educational change and influence the way it turns out. As it suggests, change is always a mix of broader forces and the interaction of individuals with them. People, individually or in combination, shape these broader forces and factors in order to influence the way

7

Table 1.1   Change sources and influences

External

Conditions	Procedures	Key players
1 Societal trends	1 Change management	1 Politicians and advisers
2 Relationships between key bodies (especially in funding areas)	2 Administrative	2 Accreditation bodies
3 Resource position of clients/students	3 Communication	3 Employers
4 Clients' learning requirements	4 Decision making	4 Granting bodies
5 Government policy		5 Unions
		6 Professional bodies
		7 Parent organisations (in the school sector)
		8 Lobby groups

Organisation

Conditions	Procedures	Key Players
1 Social conditions (culture and climate)	1 Change management	1 CEO and senior staff
2 Prior change experiences	2 Administrative	2 Central administrative staff
3 Structure	3 Communication	3 Council/governing body
4 Financial position	4 Decision making	4 System wide liaison staff/project managers
5 Policy requirements	5 Staff selection and support	
6 Appropriateness and clarity of mission	6 Dissemination of good practice	5 Union representatives
	7 Record systems	

Local

Conditions	Procedures	Key players
1 Social conditions (culture and climate)	1 Change management	1 Local unit head
2 Prior change experiences	2 Administrative	2 Local administrative staff
3 Structure	3 Communication	3 Department heads
4 Financial position	4 Decision making	4 Manager of each innovation team
5 Policy requirements	5 Staff selection and support	
6 Appropriateness and clarity of mission	6 Dissemination of good practice	5 Staff
	7 Record systems	6 Learners

in which a change effort turns out. Depending on the type and size of a change, politicians, senior bureaucrats, industry executives, unions, professional groups, key committees, institutional leaders, local managers, teachers, students and the general community may all play a role. The way in which these people relate to each other, the culture, morale and the standard operating approach of the institution they populate will all influence the outcomes of the change process.

Table 1.1 also demonstrates that, whereas some educational improvements or innovations may be entered into voluntarily by a local unit or institution, many may be forced on educators by an outside funding body. This is because education is always at the behest of the government or other external funding groups. Many of the major changes in education over the past years have come from the interaction between a change forced by a new government and the attempts of the local system and institutions to accommodate it.

Different types of change

In education there are two major types of change: changes in learning programs and changes in the milieu in which these are developed, delivered and supported.

The following list summarises some of the major aspects of learning programs which can be changed:

- learning objectives and content;
- teaching and learning strategies;
- learning resources;
- the sequencing of learning;
- learning procedures;
- learning locations and modes of learning;
- approaches to learner recruitment and participation;
- approaches to evaluation and enhancement;
- administration;
- timing and flexibility of learning;
- fee structures.

This next list summarises some of the major ways in which the operating milieu of education can be changed:

- culture and climate;
- staff selection and support;

- leadership;
- approach to identifying and disseminating good practice;
- systems of communication;
- administrative focus and procedures;
- structure;
- approaches to monitoring and enhancing organisational operation;
- documentation and statistic keeping;
- planning and decision making;
- resource distribution.

There is a close relationship between what is outlined in these two lists. In any change effort, learning program innovations will usually require some adjustment to the operating milieu if they are to be effectively supported. For example, one of the reasons why many intrinsically worthwhile and well shaped learning program innovations founder is because administrative and support personnel are either unaware of or unwilling to make the necessary behavioural adjustments to support the smooth implementation of the innovation. Again, a change from week-by-week class attendance to a mixed, intensive mode of learning may well require administrative changes in regard to room allocations and timetabling. It may also require more rapid processing of learning results. Similarly, a move to use interactive web-based learning will require information technology staff to deliver the hardware and software support systems necessary to ensure that users find access easy and reliable.

Changes in scope, size and condition

The scope and size of educational change efforts can vary dramatically. For example, some learning program innovations might simply entail a teacher enhancing one aspect of a teaching session, like introducing a new way of using a learning resource. Others, however, can be far more ambitious involving, for instance, many teachers in a complete course restructure or the introduction of a quite different means to deliver a course. This may involve them in considerable degrees of innovation in areas such as work-based learning, self-managed learning or interactive uses of the internet.

Similarly, some educational changes might affect only one location (for example, one school, college, training unit or university) whereas others may have system-wide implications. Some educational changes are enhancements of existing practices, whereas others are complete innovations.

In terms of condition, some changes have already been tried, 'debugged' and enhanced in one location to provide educators in other locations with a sound working model as a starting point. Others are untested, ground breaking and the staff involved will find themselves entering completely uncharted territory.

Such variability in the size, scope and condition of educational changes explains, in part, why the process is so complex and how 'silver bullet' approaches to change management can never work.

Motivation: the human dimension of change

An understanding of what motivates individuals to engage in and stick with a change effort is central to ensuring that a desired change is successfully implemented and sustained. Three key influences on educators' motivation to get involved in and sustain a change effort must be taken into account.

Individual influences

The role which individuals play in education will, in part, shape their interest in and expectations of a particular change. Senior managers are held accountable for different things and have different roles from teachers or learners and these factors help shape their expectations and the 'success indicators' given priority by them in each change effort. The influence of role on the individual's perception of 'efficacy' (capacity for influence) in the change process has already been noted in discussing educators' change analogies (see p. 8).

The level of job security can also influence commitment to change. In a period in which there are increased redundancies in some sectors of education, different levels of commitment to change are more likely than in periods of full employment.

An individual's reasons for seeking to work in education can also play a part. For example, some people regard their work as only a minor component in a complex and varied life; others may see it as central. Family and other obligations can also shape people's reactions when change is in the air. Similarly, assumptions as to the purpose of education vary widely and influence the way in which individuals react to different change proposals. This is something explored in Chapter 2 when the 'Five "tribes" of education' are discussed.

Stage of career can be an influence too. People new to education may have different things on their mind to those who have been in the job for many years. This partially explains why some change analogies talk of 'whitewater rafting' or being on an 'icy slide' whereas others talk of 'swamp negotiation'.

The commitment of individuals to a specific change is always influenced positively if the local manager and senior staff publicly anoint the change, noting that developing such change is a priority for them and that funds to support the effort are being committed to its success.

Not only when a change idea is first introduced, but also as it is developed, implemented and monitored each of the individuals involved in it will be continuously asking questions like the following:

- Is this *feasible*? That is, considering the apparent size and scope of what is involved, do I have time to get or stay involved in this development given all my other commitments? Does it look like we have the resources to make this work? What will we be getting rid of in my work-load in order to make room for this innovation?
- Is this *relevant*? That is, does this look like it will be met with a positive response from my students, employers and other interested players?
- Is this *desirable*? That is, does this development align with

my goals for education, with what I believe constitutes valuable education?

■ Is what is being proposed *clear*? That is, do I understand what I will have to do differently in order to make the proposed change work in practice? Am I getting consistent messages about this innovation?

If the answers to such questions are predominantly negative then individuals' motivation to persevere with the change effort will fade away.

How the change process itself is handled

Individuals may start off with a positive response to the above questions but, because the change process itself is poorly handled, their enthusiasm for the particular change may wane.

For example, there are many instances of initially promising change projects where the team involved met endlessly and aimlessly discussing what to do and finally became so exhausted that they had no energy left to put anything new into practice. Well meaning people asked to lead a change effort can quickly turn off motivation if they ignore guidelines for effective start-up strategies and support for implementation such as outlined in Chapter 2.

As implementation proceeds, the motivation of those who are to make the change work in practice will soon fall away if they are left unsupported, if inevitable implementation glitches are brushed aside by managers, anticipated resources fail to turn up on time and so on.

Similarly, if evaluation occurs too quickly or is too judgmental when it is discovered that all has not worked out as anticipated, then staff will become disheartened and commitment will wane.

Overall, if people find that the cost to them continues to be outweighed by the benefit they are more likely to persevere with a change effort. If the opposite holds they will disengage.

Influence of the local operating milieu

People may be initially motivated to tackle a given change and yet still find that, due to a counterproductive or unsupportive workplace, staff enthusiasm for the change fades as the change process gets underway.

For example, in research reviewed by Ball (1987) and Scott (1990) numerous cases were identified where the efforts of an enthusiastic local change group were 'white-anted' by other 'rival' groups in the local workplace, where the local head was uninterested in their efforts, where the culture was conservative, blaming and negative, where there was little positive recognition and reward for successful change and where the local operating processes were so inefficient that the change effort stalled. Every workplace has its own psychological history and this, in part, explains current levels of interest in improvement and innovation.

It is important when studying the change process therefore not just to look at how best to develop, implement and monitor a learning program innovation (see Chapter 2) but to concurrently understand how best to develop a workplace milieu conducive to continuous quality improvement and innovation (see Chapter 3).

The exact way in which motivation and change in education are linked is still comparatively unstudied, especially in areas of post-secondary education like training, community education and higher education.[8]

Evaluation

Evaluation is 'the process by which individuals make judgments of worth about an innovation, a process, procedure, project or strategy'.[9] It is the driving force of the change process. It is often falsely assumed that evaluation is simply something which happens at the end of a course or through formal mechanisms like student satisfaction surveys. In fact evaluation, especially informal evaluation, takes place right from the outset of any change effort. It is the engine-house of change and individual values and motives are its fuel.

It is through ongoing evaluation that people determine if a proposed change is still, from their perspective, feasible, relevant, desirable or clear. It is through evaluation that people make judgments about whether or not the change process is being well handled or whether the milieu in which the change is being attempted is sufficiently supportive to warrant putting effort into making it happen. Every person involved in a change effort is continuously gathering evidence with which to make judgments about such matters. Their judgments determine how they react. If, for example, individuals conclude that a particular change is no longer feasible or that it is being poorly managed and supported then their motivation to stick with it can fall away. On the other hand, if they come to the opposite conclusion, commitment to persevere with the process is enhanced.

It is very important to remember that such a process is not, as emphasised above, a one-off matter. It is ongoing. Evaluation occurs when an idea for change is first proposed, it occurs as innovations are designed, and it continues to take place as they are being implemented. If tapped positively, ongoing evaluation is the key mechanism for ensuring that an initiative is subject to continuous quality improvement. And it is ongoing evaluation that is both influenced by and shapes motivation.

Evaluation is reciprocal. That is, evaluation at one point in time can dramatically influence behaviour at another. And the judgments made can be surprisingly durable. For example, staff involved in a failed change project can remember this experience for years, often refusing to become involved in subsequent projects because of it.

It is naive in the extreme to assume, therefore, that the formal, documented processes of evaluation are necessarily the most significant aspect of the process. Instead it is usually the informal, ongoing, micropolitical side of evaluation that is most telling. In this hidden side of organisational life different, rival groups make judgments about each call for change not necessarily by looking at the intrinsic merits of the idea but by making judgments about the people proposing it. When micropolitics are at play the change effort can stall simply because one subgroup concludes that, since the idea is being put forward by another subgroup regarded as being inept, untrustworthy or of the 'wrong' educational persuasion, it should be dismissed out of hand.

The whole area of evaluation and micropolitics is such a vital ingredient in the change process in education that it is given detailed consideration in the following chapter.

PUTTING THE PIECES TOGETHER: A FRAMEWORK FOR UNDERSTANDING AND WORKING WITH CHANGE

Figure 1.1 summarises the discussion to date.

This view of how educational change and its management operate can be explained as follows. External (D), organisational or local influences (B) can all play a role in triggering a change effort and in determining how it turns out. Changes are possible in an educational organisation's milieu (B) or in its learning programs (C). These changes can be enhancements (that is, improvements in the quality of existing aspects of an organisation's milieu or learning programs) or they can be innovations (the introduction of something completely new).

Changes in learning programs will often generate a need to make adjustments in their operating milieu. As a general rule, for change management to be effective and efficient, changes in (B) and (C) should be explicitly linked, with the initial focus being on continuous improvement and innovation in learning programs and the implications for enhancements or innovations in milieu arising out of these learning developments. Changes in the milieu which do not demonstrably add value to the quality of learning program design and delivery should be avoided.

There is extensive research now available on what optimises the success of learning program innovations and enhancements in such an environment. This is reviewed in Chapter 2. We also now know far more about what sort of organisational

Figure 1.1   Change management framework for education

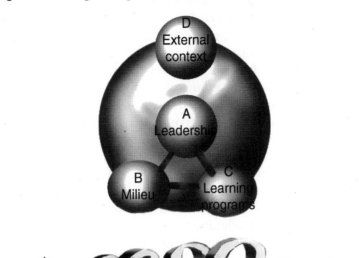

Cycles of change over time

climate, culture, structure, approach to staffing, communication and decision making best supports learning program innovation, enhancement and delivery. This research is reviewed in Chapter 3. A key tool, characteristic of the 'learning organisation' which can be used to continuously enhance workplace milieu, is workplace action research. This is discussed in Chapter 4.

Given the volatile and infinitely variable context in which education must operate, the aim should be to engage in an ongoing process of 'mutual adaptation',[10] a process in which the external context (D) or current experiences with learners may indicate a learning enhancement or innovation (C) and, from these developments, the changes in (B) necessary to support their efficient and effective implementation are identified. The approach must be cyclical not linear as, over time, constant movement in the local, organisational and external environment will necessitate continuous adjustment, enhancement or innovation in both learning programs and milieu.

The ongoing challenge is, therefore, to figure out how best to maintain synergy between B, C and D. As there are always going to be more change possibilities than there is time to deliver them, priorities will have to be set, monitored and, when necessary, adjusted. In order to set priorities, close consideration of what is going to be most feasible, relevant, desirable and strategically significant is necessary.

Right from the outset the driving force of change is people—their motives, histories, learned ways of behaving, perceptions and relationships. If an organisation or unit is populated by people who are disaffected, who feel uninvolved, unappreciated, unsupported or who are unwilling to embrace change, then even the most committed leaders in the world will have difficulty gaining their commitment for educational reform.

The change management approach which has been found to best account for the complexity outlined in this chapter and summarised above involves not taking an either–or position but combining apparently paradoxical tactics. These include the adoption of both:

- top-down and bottom-up strategies;
- an internal and an external focus;
- pan-institutional developments and uniquely local ones;
- clear direction and flexibility;
- stability and change;[11]
- enhancement and innovation;
- learning program changes and milieu enhancements;
- attention to learning program change and associated administrative/support system change;
- an emphasis on implementation support as well as development support;
- attention to resistors and enthusiasts.

Educational changes do not unfold spontaneously—they have to be led (A). Depending on the nature and scope of the change, different people may take on the role of change leader. For example, a staff member who is already expert in running interactive web-based learning may be the best person to lead a team whose job it is to spread the innovation across the organisation. For a policy innovation, a more senior staff member who is accountable for this work might be better positioned to lead the development. There are effective change leaders and ineffective ones. In Chapter 5 the research on effective ones is reviewed. What is clear is that the best leaders don't just possess requisite skills and knowledge; they are particularly sensitive to people's motives, they understand the human, subjective side of change and operate contingently by being able to 'read' and 'match'. Of particular significance is the recurring finding that the most effective leaders have a profile remarkably similar to the best teachers of adults.

As the external context (D) in which educational services must operate is continuously changing, it is essential to look not just within the organisation for change ideas but outwards and forwards. This issue is explored in detail in Chapter 6.

PUTTING THIS FRAMEWORK TO THE TEST

It is important to test out if this framework and the theory of change which underpins it are of practical use and to figure out if what is proposed helps make sense of change in the complex reality of daily life in education. It is for this reason that the following fictional case study has been included.

Pacific Institute for Higher Education's 'Blueprint for Renewal'

Pacific Institute for Higher Education (PIHE) is a large multi-campus organisation providing diploma and degree programs in the arts and sciences for a range of professions. For many years it has had a formidable reputation for providing relevant, high quality learning programs and undertaking applied research in a range of disciplines. Over this time student demand for its courses and research funding has been consistently high.

For the past two years, however, PIHE's recurrent funding from usual sources has been reduced, staff have sought and won pay increases and there has been a drop in demand for a number of courses in the arts and sciences. Harder times across the higher education sector have resulted in increased levels of competition between PIHE and its neighbouring institutions for both local and overseas students and for research funds. Recent government policy changes have allowed prestigious overseas institutions to recruit local students into their programs and to set up local offices. These overseas institutions have a high level of funding available and are already delivering programs using the Internet.

Recently, a new president, Professor Shift, has been appointed at PIHE. Professor Shift has been specifically charged by PIHE's governing council with ensuring that PIHE positions itself to succeed and expand its 'market share' in the new environment. The new president comes with a reputation as an innovator.

In a series of visits to faculties and units, the new president encounters varying degrees of enthusiasm for the need to reform. In some locations staff already have a range of relevant innovations and enhancements underway and enthusiastically discuss how these will assist PIHE in the new environment. In other locations the president encounters outright hostility, distrust, fear or silence.

It is decided that a task force for reform at PIHE be established. It is led by Professor Shift and comprises a range of carefully selected senior staff from different faculties and support units. A wide range of consultations with staff are held and the task force produces a 'PIHE Blueprint for Renewal'. The key changes identified include the development of more flexible approaches to learning, a new fee structure and a more aggressive search for new markets and funding sources both inside and outside Australia.

These change priorities are then supported with earmarked funds and assistance from a range of PIHE support and administration units is made available.

After twelve months it is clear that some departments have made considerable strides, whereas others appear to have achieved little. In a number of cases there are complaints about the unresponsiveness of central support and administrative units and their failure to provide practical assistance or to change traditional approaches.

Professor Shift commissions a workplace survey and comments like the following emerge:

What's happening to us? The whole place is being turned into a business. This isn't higher education.

I don't know what they are on about. In our section we've always been flexible.

Finally we've got some real leadership and we know where we're going. It's great.

I don't know about the other departments but we're getting a real buzz out of this. We've succeeded in getting a number of flexible learning programs up. I suppose it's because we've been hand-picked by our head of department and get on so well together.

I really object to being forced to fit in with their agenda. What do they know about how hard it is out here just to keep things going, let alone add all these innovations on top? What are we talking about, that's what I want to know.

Nice idea but sorry, no time.

All we've got is a plan and we're meant to get on with it. My question is how? We don't even know where to start.

I'm just going to let them rattle on while I just continue doing what I've always done. I've seen it all before.

I can see we've got to do something, otherwise we mightn't even have a job. But the problem is what? There's

21

just too many possibilities that might work. We're paralysed by choice.

Here in the enrolment section all we seem to be getting is abuse. We want to help but they won't spend the time to sit down and tell us how. And they don't seem to understand how hard it is.

No comment. I've only got a couple of years until retirement. It's your vision, not mine.

We've had endless meetings and talk-fests but nothing's changed yet.

What's happened to the sorts of things I thought we stood for at PIHE—critical thinking, creating new ideas, critiquing government policy not just accepting it? Now we are simply getting into bed with industry and commerce and doing their training for them.

I'm tired of blind idealism. The harsh reality is if we don't get money we lose our jobs.

Show me the rewards and then I'll put some time into it.

If we didn't have to work with that department over there we'd be surging ahead. All they do is block everything and white-ant whatever we do. It's pathetic, why doesn't someone do something about them?

If we didn't have all that money being creamed off by the centre, we'd have plenty of resources to get on with what we want to do.

- What does this case study say about the way in which the change process in education works? In particular what aspects of the process must be understood and handled effectively if any change effort is to succeed?
- What does the case tell us about the role that value judgment plays in the change process?
- How authentic is the case study compared with your experience of change? What is missing? What rings true?
- How well does the theory of change proposed in

the earlier sections of this chapter account for this case?

■ Given the scope of the challenge faced by Professor Shift, how well was this change project handled? What was done well and what might have been done differently?

CONCLUSION

If the complexity of the change management process in education is to be understood and practitioners are to be assisted in identifying practical ways to address the challenges it poses, it is vitally important that they develop an overall framework with which to make sense of what is happening when change is in the air. In other words, they need to be able to see how the many aspects of their daily experience with change in education fit together into one big picture.

This framework must address the complex dynamics of the process, link the range of activities and services which make up an education service, take account of numerous change management myths which have arisen in recent years, be uniquely suited to the distinctive operating context of education and embody the central roles played by motivation, values and evaluation.

In Chapter 1 such a framework has been developed and is summarised in Figure 1.1. The rest of this book explores the components of this framework in detail, seeking to identify practical ways of acting on the lessons learned from it. By utilising it when they inevitably become involved in change projects, educators should feel less victims of mysterious forces which they can't understand or connect. As a consequence, they should find themselves better equipped to really make a difference with the changes they take on.

What are the central lessons which emerge from this

chapter? First, that it is important to accept that the change process in education is inevitably going to be uncertain, ongoing, cyclical, reciprocal, and that it always involves a mix of individual initiative and having to cope with forces beyond one's control. Second, that it is highly subjective, with a combination of values, evaluation and individual motivation driving the way in which each initiative unfolds, right from the first moment a change idea is mentioned. Third, that individual, educational and organisational change are all linked. Fourth, that intentional change does not happen spontaneously but must be led. Finally, because of the first four lessons, it is important to be wary of a range of simplistic change management myths which have arisen in recent years: the knight on the white charger myth; the consensual myth; the linear myth; the brute logic myth; the change event myth; the silver bullet myth; the one size fits all myth and the either/or myth.

As this chapter has emphasised, there are two main types of change which educators must be deft at handling: those to do with learning programs and those associated with the organisational milieu or environment in which these learning programs must operate. It is to the detailed exploration of good practice in handling the former area that we now turn.

2

—

MANAGING CHANGE IN LEARNING PROGRAMS

This chapter outlines and illustrates the contingent and cyclical nature of the learning program change process. Practical checkpoints for effective management of different phases of program change are summarised and a case study is used to apply and test out these checkpoints and the strategies advocated. Key concepts and terms relevant to the program innovation and enhancement process are defined and discussed and an overview of what is involved in the programming process given. Components common to all learning programs are identified and the many options for handling each component are noted. Particular emphasis is given to the cyclical rather than linear nature of the programming process.

The chapter also includes a review of research on effective start-up tactics for program innovation. Practical change management checkpoints for this phase cover the effective involvement of key players, efficient ways of generating programming ideas and testing them for their desirability, relevance, distinctiveness, feasibility and clarity.

Research on effective support during the implementation of learning program innovations is also reviewed. The chapter looks at the development and use of a positive program climate as a support mechanism, effective approaches to staff learning, the use of 'executive mentors' to secure support for the change, and key negotiation tactics.

In the light of research on effective approaches to program evaluation and its use for continuous enhancement an evaluation framework for program innovations is proposed. The important role of informal evaluation and micropolitics is noted, and an efficient and comprehensive approach to evaluation planning is illustrated.

It is important to be clear on the meaning of two key concepts before getting down to the detail of this chapter, 'learning programs' and 'curriculum'.

A 'learning program' is defined as a sequence of learning activities which is developmental, linked and focused on producing desired changes in learner attitudes, ways of thinking, skills or knowledge.

Effective 'learning program design' is defined as a process:

- *which takes into account* the background, abilities, needs and experiences of students, the views of experts, accreditation requirements and available resources
    - *in order to produce* a feasible combination and sequence of content, learning strategies, resources and locations, assessment methods and administrative arrangements
        - *with the prime purpose of* optimising relevant student learning in order to achieve agreed goals and objectives.

The difference between a learning program and a learning session is, therefore, mainly a question of degree. To design a learning session one has to do much the same work as designing a learning program but the focus in the latter case is more complex because of the need to sequence and link individual learning sessions appropriately.

The term 'curriculum' is often used to describe a course of study. In this sense it can be seen as being interchangeable with the term 'learning program'. However, for many people, the term curriculum is typically associated with a pre-set and accredited course of study rather than one which is negotiated with the learner. The term learning program can cover both cases.

THE PROCESS OF LEARNING PROGRAM INNOVATION AND ENHANCEMENT

The process of learning program innovation and enhancement requires skill in 'reading and matching'. This 'contingent' approach to learning program development requires the design team to be able to 'read' what will be most desirable and relevant to each new group and situation and 'match' that combination of learning options which is most appropriate and feasible. It is practitioners' skill in 'reading and matching' at the design stage which helps determine how well a program innovation or enhancement will turn out once it is put into practice.

To effectively 'read and match' a guiding framework is necessary. This is a map which identifies where to look and what options and factors must be considered. Figure 2.1 likens the challenge of designing and implementing a learning program innovation to the process of negotiating an educational 'swamp', a place capable of continuous movement and variability. The challenge is to take into account (read) the exact character and state of the many 'islands' in each new learning context encountered, and to match a plan of action which best fits these conditions. Doing so requires a well developed knowledge of the many learning tools and design options that are possible and, once a particular design is decided upon, a capability to deliver them competently.

This analogy suggests that, as the process of 'reading and matching' takes place, it is wise both to keep an eye on external conditions and to seek out and learn from people negotiating similar programming situations elsewhere. It acknowledges that once a particular learning situation is entered, that is, once implementation of a selected plan of action commences, unexpected changes in conditions or a discovery that some factors had been 'misread' may warrant a change of direction (a program enhancement). It is during implementation, therefore, that the tactics of continuous quality improvement (CQI) come into play. Finally, each time a particular learning 'swamp' is left, that is, after program

Figure 2.1 The education programming swamp

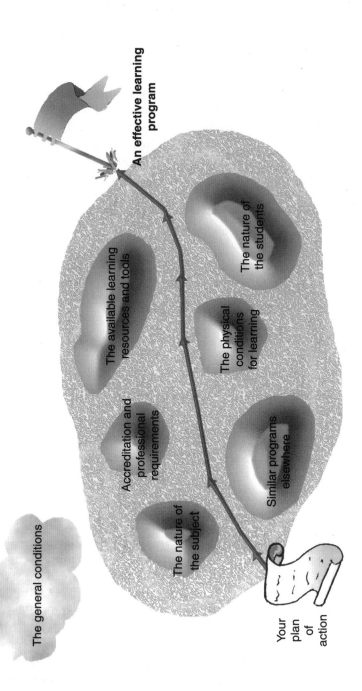

The general conditions

The nature of the subject

Accreditation and professional requirements

The available learning resources and tools

The physical conditions for learning

The nature of the students

Similar programs elsewhere

Your plan of action

An effective learning program

implementation has been completed, the practitioners involved should reflect on the experience, seeking to identify what they would or would not do again when a similar group of learners and conditions are encountered.

In the rest of this chapter practical suggestions from educators previously successful at negotiating the program change process are given. In order to manage the program innovation and enhancement process effectively however, it is essential to have an overall picture of the components to be considered. Each component is capable of great variability and the way in which these can be combined varies widely also.

As noted earlier, all learning programs have a common set of components. They all focus on particular learning objectives and content. They all adopt a particular set of teaching and learning strategies, include a specific set of learning resources, have a particular sequence of learning sessions, a preferred approach to assessment, and use specific locations for learning. All have a particular approach to recruiting learners, to evaluating and monitoring what happens, and to administering the program.

Because of this, successful program designers always make sure they address the following common set of questions.

- Which *learning objectives* should guide what happens in this program?
- What content must the learning program cover?
- What teaching and learning *strategies* are most appropriate?
- What learning *resources* will best enhance these learning strategies?
- What is the most appropriate way to *sequence* learning segments?
- What *assessment* approaches and tasks should be used?
- *Where* should learning take place?
- What should be done about *recruiting and admitting* learners to the program?
- What approach to program *evaluation and monitoring* is most appropriate?
- How should the program be *administered and supported*?

29

When answering each of the above questions program designers will be faced with a wide range of options. The many different ways in which the program components listed above can be handled are identifiable. The process of designing a learning program by 'reading and matching' requires making decisions about which options within each component are most likely to achieve the program's overall goals for the client group encountered, given the limitations of the context and available resources. The quality tests to be applied to the emerging learning design should focus on determining that the combination of options being selected is the most relevant, desirable, distinctive, clear and feasible one possible (Scott, 1996c, 1997).

Design options in learning programs

Learning objectives

These can focus on knowledge, skills, attitudes or ways of thinking. They can be derived from researching 'real life' problems with learners, from textbooks, research articles or from consulting experts, professional capability profiles or fellow educators. Irrespective of how they are identified learning objectives must be clear, valid (that is, relevant and desirable) and achievable. Learning *content* is determined by deciding what information and skills will best assist learners to achieve these objectives.

Teaching and learning strategies

There are dozens of options from which to choose. These range from lectures, workshops, lab sessions, tutorials, panels, buzz groups and simulations to interactive web-based learning, learning contracts, video-conferencing or site visits.

Learning resources

These are directly linked to the teaching and learning strategies chosen. The options include computer software, models, charts, overhead projector and powerpoint presentations, the use of telephones, films, photographs or case studies, a wide range of human resources and a variety of print materials.

Sequencing learning

Learning sessions can be grouped into discrete 'modules' or carefully linked. Sessions can be organised into a hierarchy; they can move from the simple to the complex. The sequence of learning can be fixed or negotiable.

Assessment

Assessment can be criterion referenced or norm referenced. It can use a wide range of approaches including written assignments and tests, practicum observations, portfolio presentations, experiments, research reports, analysis of work-place performance and so on.

Learning location and mode(s)

Teaching and learning can occur at one or a mix of locations and in a variety of modes, for instance at a learning centre, on the job, in the student's home, face-to-face, by telephone, via a computer network, in large groups, small groups, one-to-one, week-by-week or in a block.

Learner recruitment and participation

Learners can be recruited by open advertising, referral or word of mouth. Access can be restricted or open. There can be specific admission criteria or none. In some programs learners can come and go as they please, in others, regular attendance is a requirement.

Program evaluation

This can be both formative and/or summative. Programs can be evaluated before, during or after implementation. Evaluation can be ongoing or one-off.

31

Administration and support

Detailed student records or only very simple ones can be kept. There can be a program coordinator who keeps a close eye on implementation or this can be left to the teacher. Someone can be charged with the responsibility for making sure that all resources are in place when needed or this can be left to the learning group concerned. Some programs include quality assurance processes and specific procedures for staff development, others do not.

Timing and flexibility

Decisions have to be made about the timing, flexibility and optimal length of each learning program, that is, the degree of subject choice that students can have, whether or not articulation with parallel programs elsewhere is to be included, which patterns of attendance would be best and how open to modification the program is going to be once it is underway. Some programs are subject to outside accreditation requirements which limit flexibility, others are not.

As suggested then, there is no one learning program design to suit all occasions. The most productive combination of content, methods, resources, sequencing and so on will always depend on 'reading' what is most likely to work in the unique operating context of each program.

Furthermore, the design settled upon cannot be viewed as being 'fixed'. Because the character of the society, the economy and the organisation in which each learning program operates along with the staff and students participating in it are continually changing, each learning program must be regularly reviewed and modified if it is to remain relevant.

Therefore, as noted in Chapter 1, the whole process of learning program change is best seen as being ongoing and cyclical rather than one-off or linear. The idea is to continuously cycle through the various phases of programming—start up and design, implementation, evaluation, back to start up—

Figure 2.2   The programming cycle in education

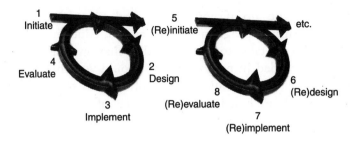

with the purpose of keeping each learning program as relevant and effective as possible.

Figure 2.2 illustrates the cyclical and continuous nature of the programming process. Program innovation occurs when a new program is considered for the first time. Program enhancement occurs when that program is redesigned in the light of what happens during implementation or as a result of a change in its operating conditions.

As Figure 2.2 suggests, the program change process, although cyclical, does entail qualitatively different phases of activity. There is a period of start up (when staff get to work on the design of a new learning program or seek to redesign an existing one). There is a different phase when the program gets underway and implementation support is necessary. Then there is the task of ensuring that the learning program is efficiently and effectively evaluated in order to determine if it is still performing up to expectations.

From a decade of research on how people manage the process of program innovation in post-secondary education (Scott, 1992a, 1996c) and in school education (Fullan, 1982, 1991) we know that the above three phases of educational programming (start up/design, implementation and evaluation) are all often handled poorly. However, we now have a clear set of guidelines (Scott, 1990; Huberman & Miles, 1984) as to what works best for each phase. It is to these findings that we now turn.

Program start up and design

What would you do if you were asked to start work on designing a learning program in your area of education? What steps would you take to optimise the chances that it subsequently succeeded in practice? Who would you involve and why? What strategies would you adopt? In this section some practical guidelines based on the practice of educators' successful learning program innovation are given.

Why this is a 'hot spot'

The reasons why many educational program innovations fail can often be traced right back to what the change team did at 'start up'. Typical errors include failure to:

- consult all the people necessary for subsequent program success early enough and/or a lack of clarity about why they were being consulted;
- take into consideration all of the program design components and options listed above;
- make sure that those for whom the program is intended— the learners—see it as being desirable, relevant and feasible;
- win the support of key administrators and support staff early on;
- check that what is planned is feasible (that is, achievable, given the resource limitations and other unnegotiable parameters set by the organisation within which the program is to be implemented);
- check that those who are to implement the program have the skills to deliver what is planned (or have the capability and the time to learn the new skills required);
- check, once the program is designed, that those who are to implement it are clear, in practical terms, on what they will do as it is being put into practice.

Effective program start-up tactics

Over the past decade considerable research has been undertaken to identify what sorts of start-up and design tactics have the most positive influence on the subsequent implementation and impact of learning programs (Fullan, 1991; Scott, 1992a). These strategies are summarised as follows. They directly address the start-up 'hot spots' identified above.

Successful learning program designers:

1 Use the checklist of program components and options outlined on pp. 30–2 to systematically guide their design of each new learning program.

2 Use a systematic process to identify what would be most desirable and relevant to the specific learning group for whom the program is intended. This typically involves interviews with people representative of the learning group, reference to capability profiles, educators running programs elsewhere with similar groups, discussions with content experts and specific reading of practitioner journals.

3 Produce a preliminary draft of a program design which, given the above input, is most likely to match the needs of the learners and the limits set by the context in which it is to be implemented.

4 Make sure key players, whose support will be needed once the program is underway, are involved by asking them to react to the draft using questions like:

- Does this program, from your point of view, seem desirable and relevant?
- Does it look feasible (achievable), given available resources?
- How could we adjust the draft program to make it better?
- What is distinctive about this draft program (different from the way we normally run programs around here)? Is it so distinctive that staff won't have the skills to implement it?
- What indicators would you use to judge that this program was ultimately a 'success'?
- What sorts of factors, actions or people could derail the program once it is underway?

- What should we do to make sure it works effectively in practice?

5 Make sure, once their draft is modified in the light of the above consultations, that the operators of the program (the teachers, learners and support staff) are clear, in practical terms, on what they will do to make sure that the program is implemented (put into practice) successfully.

The change checkpoints listed above should be referred to whenever work on a new learning program is to commence or when an existing program is being reviewed. It should be recognised that each of the tactics suggested overlaps with the others and that they don't necessarily have to be addressed in the order given. The list of strategies should be used to guide the process of 'mutual adaptation' (McLaughlin, 1976; Berman & McLaughlin, 1977) which underpins the central design task of 'reading and matching'.

The importance of covering all the components of program design

It is important, right from the outset, to keep in mind that what is to be ultimately produced is the unique combination of the program component options which best fits the unique backgrounds, abilities, needs and experience of the learners and the context in which the learning program is to be implemented.

If all of the design components and options are not considered then it is highly likely that, when the program is underway, it will be discovered that something crucial has been forgotten.

The importance of involvement

The best learning programs come about when their designers first identify all the people who will play a direct or indirect role in the learning program's subsequent operation and then appropriately involve them *early on* in the design process. There are, however, both effective and counterproductive ways of involving people in the design of learning program innovations. We now know that it is vital to make the involvement process focused, timely and brief. Endless 'program development' meetings, where no one knows why they are there or where the discussion is heading, are worse than no meetings at all. Depending on how it is handled, involvement, therefore, can be a powerful motivator or demotivator.

It is particularly important not to spend too much time getting the paperwork for a program change word perfect. It is best to adopt the tactic of 'Ready, Fire, Aim' (Peters & Waterman, 1984). The idea here is to get a picture of which program design appears to be the best fit for the given requirements and context, then to get on and try it out in practice, monitoring it closely and modifying it as you go. In this sense the most accurate documentation of the program emerges out of the process of actually putting it into practice, rather than out of its preliminary design meetings.

Consultation is a key involvement strategy. It usually proceeds best by using a limited number of carefully targeted individual or small focus group meetings. In these the views of all those affected by a change, including those who don't speak up readily in large meetings, are canvassed. Large meetings are best used to confirm that the outcomes of individual or small group consultation have been appropriately taken into account, to review a final draft of the proposed program innovation or to check that people are clear on what is actually going to happen as the program gets underway.

Who to involve and why?

A key early decision in the program design process is to identify who to consult and why getting their views is important. Everyone interviewed should have a clear interest in the particular program being designed and be in a position to make informed comment about at least one of its components. If it is not crystal clear why a meeting or interview with a particular group or individual is important, don't have it.

Some typical program change interest groups and some of the specific reasons for contacting them are listed in Table 2.1.

Effective consultation tactics

Once it has been decided who is to be consulted and why, it is important to clarify precisely what advice is to be sought

Table 2.1   Important groups to consult during start up

Target group		Reason for consulting
1 The learners (or a sample of them)	a	To assess their background, abilities, needs and experience
	b	To check that a preliminary draft program looks relevant and that their participation in it is going to be feasible
2 People who have already succeeded in the learning area under consideration	a	Those who have already 'trod the path' are seen by new learners as an excellent learning resource and model
	b	These people know the practicalities of overcoming common problems, what is most helpful and what is a waste of time
3 Colleagues (or a sample of them)	a	To supplement data on learners
	b	To identify any ways in which they might play a support role in the learning program
4 Educators elsewhere (especially ones known to run successful programs with groups of learners similar to your current target group)	a	To discover what they have found works best in similar situations
	b	To identify other people successfully involved in similar programs
	c	To identify useful learning resources, readings and articles
5 Senior managers	a	To identify unnegotiable limits (e.g. resource, policy or accreditation limits and educational priorities) within which the program must operate
	b	To identify key organisational needs and development priorities
	c	To win support for the program so that they can champion the innovation and secure support for it in senior committees
6 Content experts	a	To ensure currency, accuracy and appropriateness of all information given
7 Others:	a	. . . .
8 Others:	a	. . . .

from each group/individual. In some cases, more than one meeting may be necessary as the design process moves from gathering ideas, producing a draft design, gathering feedback on it, to finalisation. These meetings do not have to be long, provided the purpose of each meeting is clear and participants are given advance warning of the questions to be addressed. In some instances the interview can be undertaken by telephone, especially if the persons involved are well known to each other.

The following strategies have been found to work best during the meeting:

1 Confirm why the person(s) interviewed are being consulted—explain the importance of their role to the successful implementation of the program and what sorts of information they are best positioned to provide. For example:
   - With prospective students the focus would be on finding out more about their background, abilities, needs, experience, and their current problems, knowledge, skills and feelings.
   - With previous students the focus might be on how they handled the course, what tactics worked best and what ones were a waste of time. Tips for subsequent groups of learners could also be sought.
   - With a senior manager the focus might be on what sorts of organisational limitations and requirements should be taken into account, along with their success indicators, for a program of the type proposed.

2 Tell them how the information they provide will be used. Emphasise that the aim is to minimise time wasting and maximise input from them on issues about which they are in a good position to comment.

3 Make any unnegotiable limits identified by the organisation or external requirements clear—saying that their views on what would make the program work best within these unnegotiable limits is what is being sought.

4 Use the list of effective start-up strategies given on pp. 35–6 as a basis for questions.

5 Spend more time listening than talking. When talking spend less time giving your point of view, and more time asking questions aimed at gathering in further information or clarifying points being made.
6 If a lot of people have already suggested something, check the present informants' views on the desirability and feasibility of this idea.
7 Check how much time the person would have available for subsequent involvement.
8 Thank the person and go over what will happen next.

Involving learners in the design process

A particularly important group to involve in the design process is the learners for whom it is intended. In some cases direct consultation may not be feasible. In that instance it may be possible to talk with previous students or, failing this, check with educators who have run programs for similar groups elsewhere.

An ideal source of ideas is a sample of students who have already completed a similar program. They can give excellent advice on how they learnt what to do, what the key problem areas were, what was most useful and what was a waste of time. Don't underestimate the importance of getting advice from those who have already 'trod the path'.

Below are some specific guidelines on what might be emphasised if a meeting with prospective or past students becomes possible.

Identify the particular backgrounds, abilities, needs and experiences of the learners

Seeking to 'read' these is significant because it gives important clues on how each of the program components and options might best be handled.

For example, different backgrounds, experiences and learning styles can dictate the adoption of different learning strategies, levels of difficulty in reading materials, different learning locations, and different content emphases. Different abilities (for example, differing levels of cognitive functioning or loss of dexterity with age) may dictate the adoption of different class groupings, resources and paces of learning. Different emotional needs and developmental stages will also influence the learning tactics adopted.

Identify the target group's current concerns, including perceived gaps in knowledge and skill

A problem-based approach to learning program design (Boud & Feletti, 1991) has been found to be one very useful way to ensure that learning objectives and content are immediately relevant to learners. For example, when the program is work-related, the key problems and dilemmas encountered there can become a rich and relevant source of learning.

> In place of traditional classroom based approaches to training, the focus shifts to the learning potential of everyday work activities. From the new perspective, employees are recognised as active participants in the learning process and a whole range of workplace experiences—participation in decision-making, developing learning resources, teamwork, undertaking new assignments, mentoring, even dealing with controversy and crises—are seen as opportunities for learning. (L. Field in Foley, 1995: 163)

The focus here is, therefore, on identifying what currently is causing each new group of learners most concern. This will enable the particular gaps in knowledge and skills that should be given priority in the learning program to be specified.

In the case of workplace learning programs, attention to workers' learning needs in relation to the development priorities and requirements of the organisation is also important. In such a situation, identifying the organisation's desired outcomes and development priorities and using a process of 'backward mapping' (Elmore, 1979) towards a learning design which meets these needs is a key tactic.

It should be borne in mind, however, that learners may not necessarily be able to 'express their learning needs' or to identify the exact nature of the problems they are facing. Nor should they necessarily be expected to label exactly what their knowledge and skill gaps are. The best tactic is to keep in mind common problems previously experienced by similar groups of learners and go about trying, with the learner's assistance, to diagnose what educational input seems to be most needed. Problems and areas for development can occur in any or all of the following:

- the learner's stance;
- the learner's knowledge;
- the learner's skills;
- the learner's way of thinking.

A detailed discussion of each of these four aspects of competence and their educational implications is undertaken in Scott (1996c, 1997).

Other sources of ideas

Although people are a key source of ideas for what might best be included in a new learning program, there are other sources which can also be helpful.

Books and journals (especially those which are targeted specifically on the areas being dealt with in the learning program under development) can be an important resource. The art of using these effectively is similar to the art of consulting people effectively: don't randomly read, always try to identify a book or journal which has ideas on one or more of the program components and which, if possible, is also about the target group for whom the program is being designed.

Photographs, films and video clips of educators working with learning groups or in a one-to-one situation can also be a useful source of ideas. Once again, the aim is to locate only the most relevant resources.

Last, but not least, the program development team's own previous experience with similar learning groups is an important source.

Creating a preliminary 'draft' of the learning program innovation

When the data gathered in the ways suggested above have been brought together into a preliminary program design, it is then time to document what is proposed. The following guidelines suggest one format for documenting a learning program. What is produced should be brief—about four or five pages.

1 Program title
2 Target group profile
  Number of learners involved
  Range of backgrounds, abilities, needs and experience
  Key knowledge and skill gaps
  Aspects of stance and way of thinking to be addressed
3 Overall program goal(s)
4 Unnegotiable limits within which the program must operate
  Resource limitations (people, money, facilities)
  Policy requirements
  Professional requirements
  Accreditation requirements
5 Learning system
  For each learning area:
  Learning objectives: 'On completion of this area of learning students will be able to . . .'
  Assessment tasks, strategies and criteria
  Key content
  Key learning activities and their sequence
  Learning resources and infrastructure necessary to support learning activities
  Learning location(s)
  Approximate time needed for teaching and learning
6 Proposed recruitment strategy/criteria
7 Program management and administrative requirements
8 Proposed evaluation tactics and timing
9 Key implementation support/requirements to be addressed

This overall program profile can then be used to guide the development of the individual session plans that make up each learning area, as well as the development of an implementation support and evaluation plan.

Check the draft learning design with key players

Once a draft proposal for the learning program is produced feedback should be sought from the key players already contacted. The focus here is on inviting people to react to the quality of the draft learning program from their perspective, commenting on its desirability, relevance, feasibility, distinctiveness and clarity. The aim is to further improve the program's chances of 'success' given the profile of the learner group for which it is intended and the limitations under which it must operate.

Check for desirability

Is this program design likely to achieve the learning outcomes most valued by the institution, staff, the professions it serves and other relevant players? Are the outcomes perceived to be desirable by the various people involved? Is the design consistent with what we know about effective teaching and learning?

Keep in mind that people in different roles may see desirability from the perspective of their role as well as from their own perspective on what constitutes a valuable educational experience.

Check for relevance

Does this program design match the specific backgrounds, abilities, needs and experience of the students who are to undertake it? Are the capabilities being developed specifically relevant to what employers, higher level courses of study or the professions require?

Check for feasibility

Can what is outlined in the draft program be achieved given the current quality of infrastructure, support systems, facilities, staffing profile and policy limitations? If not, can the resources be found to upgrade them in the ways required or should the proposed design itself be 'downsized' to make it workable? If 'downsizing' is necessary, how can the idea be modified to make it workable without losing its most desirable elements?

Remember that the feasibility (achievability) of the plan can be influenced by external, system or local factors (see Chapter 1). For example, if the proposal aligns with government or organisational funding priorities then feasibility is enhanced. If the local milieu is supportive feasibility is also enhanced.

Check for distinctiveness

Asking about what components of the proposed plan appear distinctive (that is, different from past practice, new to the people who are to implement them) gives another angle on feasibility. It is no good having a highly relevant, innovative and interesting learning program if staff don't have the knowledge or skills to make it work in practice. It may be possible to fill these gaps through staff development, especially by linking up with educators who have already successfully implemented similar innovations elsewhere. If this is not possible it is important to make sure that staff feel capable of developing the new ways of doing things as the program is implemented. If such strategies do not appear possible then the proposal may need further modification until its implementation becomes achievable.

Check for clarity

Here the focus is on whether or not everyone who has a role in the program is clear on what, in practical terms, they will do when the program gets underway. It is possible for people to be clear on what they must do but to remain unclear on how to do it. In this case they will either need direct implementation support or pre-implementation training or, as noted above, the program will have to be modified (downsized) to match their current skills and knowledge.

Finalise the program plan

Once feedback on the draft program plan has been received, the innovation should be finalised by converting it into an action plan. Note that this action plan should be seen as a map for initial implementation not as something which must be adhered to rigidly. As noted earlier in this chapter, the programming process is cyclical and further modifications to the program design should be expected in the light of what happens as it is put into practice and monitored. In general, the more ambitious and distinctive the innovation, the more modification during early implementation is to be expected.

If the program is to be submitted for accreditation it will be necessary to adapt the draft to fit the format set by the accrediting authority.

Key change management tactics at start up

The tactics for the start-up stage of program innovation or enhancement outlined above align with the change research reviewed in Chapter 1. For example, they take into account the fact that:

- program innovation is a cyclical process not a linear one;
- what is done at start up dramatically influences how well the innovation turns out when it is put into practice;
- failure to involve key players (for example, learners, teachers, administrators) early on can result in failed change later;
- failure to use 'best practice' frameworks to guide the development of an innovation can result in inefficiency, discontent and difficulties during implementation;
- failure to ensure that what is developed is not just desirable

but also feasible (achievable) can result in significant problems during implementation;

- the process of change is a very subjective thing—it concerns values, micropolitics, people's goals, interests and perceptions. In any group of change players, assumptions and interests will vary considerably depending on each person's role, 'tribal perspective' and past history within the organisation;

- the hardest phase of change is making an innovation work in practice, not planning or pre-specifying and documenting it in minute detail;

- the process of innovation is always a mix of individual action (what people can do to influence outcomes) and drift (the influence of forces and factors beyond the control of individuals);

- learning from those who have already 'trod the path' in the change area being embarked upon is a key tactic. This requires being effective at identifying and using practitioner networks effectively. 'Piggybacking' an innovation onto existing ones within and beyond the organisation (Bush & Bock, 1982) is an important aspect of this.

Below is a case study of a learning program innovation of considerable scope and challenge.

Austec: start-up strategy for a flexible learning program innovation

Austec is a large national manufacturing company with some 800 employees. Continuous change in its markets and in technology, combined with the effects of the international recession, leads the Austec Board to look for the most cost-effective ways of continuously updating the competence of all its employees in order to remain competitive. In general, the Board has concluded that the company's traditional approach of running two-day training workshops for employees in different work categories once or twice a year is not achieving this goal. They also decide that the costs associated with paying for travel and accommodation to attend these off-the-job events, along with lost productivity, can no longer be justified.

Austec's chief executive officer has recently travelled overseas to identify successful workplace learning innovations in partner companies. The CEO is especially impressed with the way in which some companies are using flexible learning strategies like mentoring programs, cross-functional action teams, web-based interactive learning and job rotation for staff development. The CEO convinces the Austec Board that it is essential that the company's training strategy adopts a more flexible and ongoing approach to workplace learning based on such innovations.

As a result, the Austec Board asks the company's Head of Training to develop, implement, evaluate and enhance a flexible workplace learning system and to consider how the innovative learning strategies identified by the CEO might best be used. The Head of Training sits down with the six trainers in her Unit to map out their change management strategy.

Given the situation outlined consider, with reference to the change checkpoints given earlier in this chapter and other relevant resources, what you would do if you were Austec's training manager to ensure that the start-up strategy for this innovation is efficient and effective and optimises the chances of its subsequent implementation being successful. Consider who you would involve and how, what you would do and what factors and conditions you would pay particularly close attention to as the process of start up for this innovation gets underway.

EFFECTIVE IMPLEMENTATION SUPPORT

Why is this a hot spot?

It is common to find that too much effort and too many resources are put into the development of learning program innovations and that too little time and effort are put into supporting them once they are underway. Overplanning and lengthy, costly development meetings are common in many organisations.

The evidence to date (Fullan, 1991; Scott, 1990, 1996c) is that the hard part in making a learning program innovation work comes *after* the program team start trying to put it into practice. This is because the context in which such programs are to be implemented is so complex and changeable that it is impossible to expect pre-packaged innovations to operate exactly as predicted, unless they are particularly simple.

The available research further identifies a number of key requirements for effective implementation support which are typically ignored or poorly handled.

- The process of implementing a learning program must be led— successful implementation does not happen spontaneously.
- There is usually little attempt to continuously and systematically monitor how an innovatory program is turning out in practice.
- Staff (and students) inevitably experience implementation difficulties but these may not surface or be dealt with. People tend to operate in isolation, feeling insecure and anxious. They receive little praise for persevering with the problems of implementation.
- Support for staff learning during implementation is usually haphazard, poorly timed and impractical. Being left to their own devices decreases staff willingness to persevere with making the innovatory components of the program work and typically results in them returning to the use of old, safe, proven strategies. Such an experience can leave them disillusioned and is likely to decrease their enthusiasm for getting involved in subsequent innovations.

- Routine administration and the organisation of needed resources can be poorly handled, further compounding the uneasiness which staff feel.
- Local program coordinators don't usually 'play the system' effectively. For instance, they often fail to keep an 'executive mentor' involved or to use organisational or external networks to sustain support for the change.
- More generally, a lack of skill in handling the micropolitics of change is common.
- The system and workplace in which the program is being put into practice needs to be willing and able to adapt its practices to support the program's implementation.

If implementation challenges like these are not deftly handled, then even the best designed program innovation will founder.

Handling these implementation 'hot spots' should not fall to one person. The ideal approach involves a small number of people working actively to identify and resolve implementation difficulties under the leadership of a program coordinator.

Research on effective implementation support

Over the past decade considerable research has been undertaken into what sorts of implementation support tactics are most effective in ensuring that a desired program innovation actually finds its way successfully into practice (Scott, 1990, 1992a, 1996c; Fullan, 1991). These tactics address the implementation 'hot spots' identified above and are summarised here. They align closely with the strategies used in the processes of Continuous Quality Improvement (CQI) discussed in Chapter 3 and Workplace Action Research in Chapter 4.

During implementation, effective learning program managers and teams:

- continuously monitor what is happening, using an agreed evaluation strategy;
- sustain a positive program climate and ensure feasible and

appropriate involvement of key players in decisions about any modifications of the program that may become necessary as a result of this monitoring;

■ give explicit attention to providing appropriate support for staff learning;

■ sustain organisational support for the program using an 'executive mentor' and informal networks;

■ are deft at reflection-in-action and on-the-spot negotiation;

■ prepare for program continuation early on.

Continuously monitor what is happening

Monitoring what happens as the program is being put into practice is vital because it is inevitable that not all of what was planned will turn out exactly as predicted. There will always be the important and unexpected twist.

The more distinctive (different from 'standard practice') various components of the learning innovation are, the more implementation difficulties and dilemmas related to these components are likely to emerge and the more likely that considerable levels of mutual adaptation will be necessary to get the program running smoothly. In carrying out the process of mutual adaptation it will be discovered that it is easier to change the learning program to fit the organisation than it is to change the organisation to better support the learning program.

In seeking to monitor the progress of an innovation, it is important to distinguish between the success of its implementation and the quality of its impact. Assessing the effectiveness of a learning program's implementation involves establishing how well the staff and students believe the change is working for them at any point in time. Assessing impact, on the other hand, involves establishing what effect all this activity is having on the perceptions and capabilities of students, staff, the local unit, the organisation and key external constituencies and interest groups. This is where an effective evaluation plan fits in, guidelines for which are given later in this chapter.

As the implementation of the learning program is monitored,

it will be necessary to remain open to unexpected but important outcomes. In fact, as implementation and impact are monitored, it may be found that some unexpected outcomes are so beneficial that the emphasis in the program should be changed to incorporate them. This reinforces a point made earlier, that what is most effective is often determined by *implementing* an innovation, not by discussing it in a planning committee.

It is important not to jump to 'summative' judgments about the quality of a program innovation's impact until it has been established that it really is operating effectively. There is a long history of managers and administrators jumping to premature conclusions about the value of a learning program innovation before it was given a chance to be refined. We have known for a long time now that it takes from three to five years for the cycles of implementation, evaluation and enhancement of a large program innovation to get it to the stage where it is operating optimally, not, as some would have us believe, six months (Fullan, 1982: 41). Even with more modest program innovations, the time needed to get them operating to everyone's satisfaction is longer than normally assumed.

Of course, it is also possible that, no matter what is done, the program just can't be made to work satisfactorily and it has to be abandoned. This, however, is a most unlikely outcome if the work at start up has been soundly carried out.

On some occasions it is possible that what is being implemented is a learning program which is 'debugged', that is, a program that has already been successfully field tested elsewhere. In this case, where there are ways of doing things that have consistently been shown to work at other sites, it may be important to insist on much greater 'fidelity' to the program plan than would be the case for an untested program. However, in our experience with program innovations, such a situation rarely holds for an overall learning program, although sometimes there may be a tried and true way of doing some of its components.

Sustain a positive program climate and continue to ensure feasible staff involvement

As noted when discussing program start-up tactics, actively involving staff in the development of the learning program heightens the chances that the final plan of action will be relevant, clear and feasible. This involvement early on also heightens key players' sense of ownership of the learning program and can develop the sort of collaborative climate necessary to help them persevere with the challenges that inevitably arise as they seek to put the program change into practice.

If colleagues, participants and other key players have a clear and agreed perspective on what the program is trying to achieve and if the program coordinator has succeeded in building an open, collaborative team-based stance towards the difficulties of implementation, then people are more likely to voice implementation problems as they arise. This will ensure that the inevitable glitches that crop up as every program change is put into practice can be overcome before they escalate. This form of informal, ongoing feedback is a key component of any effective implementation support strategy and is an important source of evaluation data. Building an open, collaborative climate is enhanced if team members see eye-to-eye, trust and respect each other and associate socially or informally. Be very wary of only using the occasional formal meeting as a mechanism for involving staff in implementation monitoring.

The local program leader's competency as a change manager is vital in developing a positive program climate, an open system of communication and in ensuring that staff involvement is effective. As will be emphasised in Chapter 3, collaborative teams must be led and built, they do not come about spontaneously. The distinctive attributes of the effective change team leader are explored in detail in Chapter 5.

Bear in mind that poorly handled approaches to staff involvement during implementation can undo all the good work undertaken at start up. For instance, poorly conceived, inadequately prepared and ineptly run staff meetings and unworkable delegation have as bad an impact on staff morale and perceptions during implementation as they do at any stage of the change process.

In general, to be effective at involving staff during implementation the local change manager must be able to clearly communicate the 'ground rules' for involvement; to quickly acknowledge contributions of staff; to delegate effectively; to balance intervention with trust; to be willing to get out of the office and into the classrooms in which the innovation is taking place, to get 'close to the customer'; to avoid overloading staff; to run effective meetings; and not to punish experimentation and unsatisfactory performance.

Support for staff learning

Effective program implementation is not an event (for example, the production of a program outline or the launch of the first session of the program). It involves a long and challenging learning (and unlearning) process, especially for the staff involved. Consequently it is vital that the program leader has the ability to appropriately use a wide variety of adult learning strategies to support staff as they gain the skills to implement the learning program and seek to put its essential components into effective practice. In this sense, as implementation proceeds, the local change leader's competence as a teacher of adults becomes increasingly important.

The timing of the support given as staff put the program plan into action is vital. Fullan (1986) and Huberman and Miles (1984) have found that the period of early implementation is the hardest and that this is when staff welcome assistance and acknowledgment of their efforts most. It can be a time of high anxiety and confusion, especially if what is being attempted represents a considerable step into new territory and if the program being attempted has many innovatory components.

The approach used to help staff learn how to implement the innovatory components of a program must be far more broadly based than simply setting up the occasional staff development 'workshop'. In fact one-off, off-the-job workshops for staff, although common, have been found to be one of the least effective implementation learning support strategies for staff.

> Simply put, most forms of inservice training are not designed
> to provide the ongoing, interactive, cumulative learning
> necessary to develop new conceptions, skills and behaviour.
> Failure to realise that there is a need for inservice work
> *during implementation* is a common problem. (Fullan, 1982: 66)

A more powerful strategy is to encourage staff to support one another informally as implementation difficulties arise. Here the change manager's skills in effective staff selection, climate building and staff involvement will be put to the test. If, as already noted, staff get along well informally and if they are encouraged to be open about implementation difficulties, then they will be more likely to help one another to resolve problems spontaneously as they occur.

Fullan's (1986) review of research on inservice education for teachers suggests that teachers like time and encouragement to exchange 'tips, war stories, encouragements, complaints, worries and requests for help' (Fullan, 1986: 9). It seems that this occurs best if it takes place early during implementation in a climate of positive informal support.

Such peer support by fellow staff should not, however, exclude other learning support strategies. For example, the change manager's skill in networking will still be important. If, during program start up, staff who are successfully implementing similar programs in other locations can be located, then a valuable resource for expanding and improving the repertoire of local staff will be available. Staff can be put into contact and both sides can be encouraged to visit, observe and comment on each other's performance. A larger gathering in which staff discuss implementation problems and successful strategies might also be organised. Either way, it is the availability of relevant, practical coaching (Joyce & Showers, 1980) on the 'nuts and bolts' of competently putting the change into practice that is important, not abstract theory isolated from the day-to-day practicalities of the innovation.[1]

More recently, developments in information technology have enabled the establishment of interactive web-sites for practitioners undertaking the same kinds of innovation in other locations and countries. This ongoing, just-in-time peer learning support is reported by practitioners as being an ideal form of implementation assistance.

There are occasions when a more formal meeting is also warranted, for instance, just before the program first gets underway to make sure everyone is clear on what they must do, how they will monitor what happens and how inevitable implementation glitches are to be handled.

The above tactics can be supplemented by self-teaching kits which bring together practical support materials and the reports of people who have succeeded in implementing particular learning innovations. It appears that it is the ability to use a combination of the above implementation learning strategies appropriately (that is, contingently and reflectively) that provides the most telling support for implementation. It is an area in which educators' skills tend to be significantly underdeveloped. This is ironical, given the fact that educational institutions are populated by people whose profession is teaching and learning.

Ensure that routine administration is effectively undertaken and that needed resources arrive on time

Depending on the particular learning innovation or enhancement under consideration and the requirements of the organisation in which it must operate, its effective implementation will, in part, depend on ensuring that all the necessary 'hackwork' is done efficiently and well ahead of time.

Ensuring that needed facilities and equipment are secured, that staff are aware of things like enrolment and learning requirements and deadlines, that staffing, timetabling and resource committees will accommodate the program's needs are all important forms of implementation support. Chapter 3 explores these institutional forms of support in more detail.

All good teaching requires high quality learning resources. If these resources are not delivered when needed during implementation then the learning program innovation will not work effectively. As noted when discussing start-up tactics, those who are to deliver the learning program should be involved in the selection and design of these materials. The construction of learning resources is, in fact, an ideal way for those who are to implement a program to work out how to put it into practice. Not all learning materials can be developed ahead of time. Individuals may very well have to design their own resources as they go along, often in response to the way in which learners are reacting and to emerging but unanticipated needs. Those effective learning strategies and resources developed during implementation need to be identified and shared. Often a few brief notes to accompany the resource is all that is needed to explain to fellow educators how it might best be used.

Use an executive mentor

As implementation proceeds, it is vital that the support of key organisational decision makers and external interest groups developed during start up is maintained. This is important because, if such people conclude that the program is 'successful' (that is, that it is meeting their identified indicators for program 'success'), they are more likely, when called upon, to support the innovation in key resourcing and decision-making committees.

It should be recognised that it is unlikely that senior managers will have an intimate appreciation of what a particular learning innovation entails or of what it is achieving because their daily work rarely gives them time to find out or observe such things. Bringing such people into contact with the daily realities of the program, especially with the students, is one tactic which can overcome this problem.

Most successful learning programs in education have such

an organisational 'mentor' or 'champion'. To be an appropriate mentor, the person chosen needs to be well respected and to have not just the power but also the informal influence to make things happen.

Deft use of on-the-spot negotiation and micropolitical networks

Underpinning all of the above implementation tasks is the need for staff to be competent in on-the-spot negotiation, especially informal negotiation. Their ability to effectively function in key external, organisational or local micropolitical networks is central to securing ongoing support for the innovation. An outline of some of the more common micropolitical strategies is given below when the influence of informal evaluation is discussed.

An ability to engage effectively in on-the-spot negotiation, often in response to a comment or situation which arises unexpectedly, is what distinguishes effective managers of the implementation process from ineffective ones. It often means the difference between a key player supporting or blocking what happens next.

These skills run throughout the entire programming process. They are necessary in order to assess demand, to determine readiness and to establish the feasibility of a proposed learning program. They are needed when clarifying what the program change might best look like in practice, to build and sustain a positive program team climate and to effectively involve staff. They are necessary to give and gain implementation support and to ensure that routine administrative tasks are efficiently carried out.

Most importantly, the skills of 'reflective negotiation' are central to ensuring that, during initial implementation, the program gets built into routine administrative and resourcing procedures, thereby securing its continuation. Doing this during, not after initial implementation, is particularly important if the learning program is being resourced with one-off funding. No matter how intrinsically worthwhile the learning program might actually be, if key senior people are unaware of it and if their specific support isn't won, then its continuation beyond initial funding is highly unlikely.

Prepare for continuation

The perspective on the program change process adopted in this book is that it is one of continuous adjustment, renewal and improvement. This was indicated earlier in this chapter when discussing the cyclical nature of the process.

Consequently, the phase of continuation is primarily concerned with ensuring that the innovation continues to remain needed and relevant, to be appropriately staffed, supported and delivered for as long as is necessary. The context in which the learning program must operate is far too turbulent for a linear or one-off approach to the process to work. Support for continuation must, as noted above, be won during early implementation. If key players have been involved right from the start gaining such support is made easier.

Take the situation outlined in the Austec case study on pp. 47–8 and assume that your suggested start-up strategy for the development of this innovation has been successful. Now, with reference to the checkpoints given in this chapter and other relevant resources, consider what you would do if you were Austec's training manager to ensure that the *implementation support* strategy for this innovation is efficient and effective and that it optimises the chances of the innovation's continuation. Consider who you would involve and how, what you would do and what factors and conditions you would give particular attention to during implementation.

LEARNING PROGRAM EVALUATION

As noted in Chapter 1, evaluation is defined as 'the process which leads to judgements about the worth, effectiveness and efficiency of an activity, project or strategy' (McDonald & Bishop, 1990: 12). Evaluation of what happens as learning programs are developed and implemented is usually haphazard.

For example, if key players in any change effort are asked how 'successful' or 'effective' a particular learning program is at any point in the process, the response received is often based on very slim evidence. It is typical to discover, furthermore, that different players are using quite different 'indicators of success' to make such judgments. There is a tendency to look to indicators concerned with the quality of a program innovation's paperwork or its efficiency rather than to more substantive ones that focus on the quality of its operation or impact.

When asked to identify and justify their preferred indicators many individuals have difficulty. Yet it is judgments based upon such indicators that profoundly influence what they choose to do (or not to do) as a learning program is being developed and implemented. For example, if it was decided that a proposed program innovation or enhancement is not needed or is not going to work, this will directly influence how much time and consideration those involved will subsequently give to it.

The lack of a shared language with which to discuss evaluation is also a problem. For example, different players often attribute quite different meanings to terms like 'evaluation' and 'learning'. This results in considerable misunderstanding as the evaluation process unfolds, with comments like 'But I thought when you said evaluate it, you meant . . .' being typical.

There are other reasons why evaluation is a program change 'hot spot'. Just as a lack of clarity about what individuals must do to support a program innovation during its implementation is a problem, so too a lack of a shared vision of how it will be judged to be 'working successfully' is common. If key players (like managers, teachers, administrators and learners) don't all know and accept the indicators that will be used to check that a program is working effectively then it will be impossible to monitor what happens as it is put into practice. It will also be difficult to identify what aspects of the program require follow-up support and enhancement.

Finally, as noted in Chapter 1, there is inadequate recognition that evaluation, especially informal evaluation, is the driving force behind the entire process of program development, implementation and improvement. It is common to equate 'evaluation' with something formal that takes place at the end of a learning program. Yet evaluation is far more pervasive and informal than this. Values, informal judgments about what is proposed and occurs are inextricably linked to what people do. This in turn determines the results of the program change effort. Evaluation and the subjective side of program design and implementation are interwoven.

Research on effective program evaluation

Over the past decade considerable research has been undertaken into what sorts of evaluation tactics and approaches contribute most effectively to the success of educational change projects (Scott, 1990, 1995a, 1995b, 1996c; Fullan, 1991). These tactics are summarised below. They directly address the evaluation 'hot spots' identified earlier.

Effective learning program evaluators:

- make sure everyone is using a shared language;
- ensure that appropriate, reliable and valid assessment tasks are built into the program;
- explicitly identify the different indicators various players intend to use to judge that the program has been 'successful' *at the outset* and attempt to accommodate these in the design and evaluation of the program;
- have a clear understanding of how the informal, micropolitical side of evaluation operates and can successfully take it into account;
- develop a comprehensive, feasible and clear evaluation plan/strategy for the program;
- effectively face and resolve common evaluation dilemmas.

It is suggested that the evaluation checkpoints listed be referred to whenever an evaluation strategy for learning program innovation or enhancement is being developed. Each of the six evaluation checkpoints is explained in more practical detail below.

Check that everyone is using the same language

Educational jargon, including evaluation jargon, can be useful provided the complex meanings for which it is shorthand are shared. However, as Popham (1993: 1) has noted, 'Once upon a time there was a word. And the word was evaluation. And the word was good . . . after a while, nobody knew for sure what the word meant. But they knew it was a good word.'

For example, how do you and your colleagues define and distinguish between the terms 'evaluation' and 'assessment'? One potentially useful way to distinguish between the two terms is as follows. Whereas 'evaluation' is the process by which judgments about the worth, effectiveness or efficiency of a particular education program are made,[2] assessment is just one of the techniques which can be used to gather data with which to make such judgments. Assessment can be of the qualities and performance of learners, teachers, resources, or programs and can vary in its validity (relevance and focus) and its reliability (accuracy).

You may not totally agree with our distinction. The point is that, whenever change is in the air, it is important for you and your colleagues to surface your assumed meanings for such terms at the start of the program change process because, if you don't, you may find out too late that you are all working at cross-purposes.

At the heart of the term 'evaluation', is the word 'value'. Making judgments of worth (attributing value) is ultimately a question, therefore, of the application of subjective perceptions of what is 'good' and 'bad'. It is in this way that we can distinguish between 'change' (to make different) and 'progress' (change in a desirable—that is, individually valued—direction).

Equally, there is confusion about what constitutes a significant outcome of the program change process. In this regard there continues to be considerable confusion about the concept of 'competence'. Some associate it with the possession of specific skills and knowledge, others give it a much more comprehensive definition. This issue is addressed in a separate paper 'Change, competence and education' (Scott, 1997) and is taken up in some detail in Chapter 4 in relation to managerial competencies. Important work in the area has been undertaken by Ashenden (NBEET, 1990) and Gonczi et al. (1990).

Build appropriate assessment tasks into the learning program

It is important to ensure that, as each new learning program is being developed, appropriate assessment tasks are built into it. It is vitally important that such tasks are both valid (that is, they tap what really makes the difference in competent performance) and reliable (that is, the methods and criteria by which performance on them will be judged are clear and consistently applied).[3] This is necessary for a number of reasons:

- What is assessed in a learning program, more than any other factor, influences what is given priority during the learning process by both teachers and learners.
- Being able to demonstrate that a learning program innovation or enhancement has consistently enhanced the quality of learning outcomes is the acid test of educational change. In order to be significant, such conclusions require that the assessment tasks upon which they are based are both valid and reliable.
- It is wrong to conclude that a learning program innovation is a 'success' because all its participants performed well on assessment tasks which were trivial.

Performance on assessment tasks, provided they are well conceived, gives vital clues not just on where learning program innovations are performing well but can identify where they may need enhancement. If, for instance, it is found that large numbers of students are failing a particular assessment task this can indicate that the segment of the learning program used to develop the capabilities tapped in that task may be poorly designed or delivered. It is in this way that learning outcomes can be used for continuous program improvement.

Identify key program 'success' indicators

Being clear about the success indicators to be used to monitor the performance of a program innovation during its implementation is most important if the support of all those involved is to be retained. These indicators can be identified when the issue of 'desirability' is explored during start-up consultations. It should be kept in mind that different players (senior staff, administrators, teachers, outside interest groups, employers, support staff etc.) are highly likely to give priority to different indicators and that they will be looking to the quality of performance on their preferred ones as implementation gets underway.

It is this range of indicators that, once surfaced and understood, should be used to formulate an appropriate evaluation and monitoring plan for the innovation. The following provides a framework with which to identify, make sense of and cluster all of the potentially relevant success indicators for a learning program change.[4]

1 *Check the quality of the program's design* For example: the clarity, feasibility and desirability of the learning program's documentation. How well it follows 'sound' adult learning and program development principles. Various sorts of written reports or the comments made by key people could be used as an indicator that it is 'soundly conceived'.

2 *Check the extent to which required resources are in place* For example: it could be determined if required equipment and learning resources were in place when needed, that teachers and students are turning up promptly, that various administrative support procedures are working.

3 *Check the extent to which operators and students are actually doing what the program documentation claims should happen* For example: the extent to which what was proposed in the learning program's documentation was actually seen by learners and teachers to be working in practice could be

established. Various sorts of survey, observation or interview methods could be used to gauge the quality of teacher performance or student satisfaction with program implementation.

4 *Check the quality of the innovation's impact on students and other key parties* For example: a variety of assessment methods could be used to determine if there has been a positive change in students' attitudes, knowledge, skills and way of thinking. In doing this it is important to ensure that both valid and reliable assessment tools are used. Other indicators could include the quality of impact the program has on participants' employment rates and careers, demand trends and the level of satisfaction with the program expressed by employers and professional associations. The impact which program participation has on the subsequent career of the staff involved could also be determined.

These guidelines have been successfully used to direct the evaluation of large· numbers of program innovations in education.[5] In using them, a number of recurring lessons have emerged.

First, indicators at levels one and two are more easily measured than ones at levels three and four. Yet outcomes at levels three and four are more significant.

Second, by regularly tapping indicators at all levels during implementation it is possible to identify areas for program improvement and modification. Poor outcomes at levels three and four automatically indicate something is awry at levels one and two. In this way having an evaluation plan based on this framework is a key pre-condition for effective ongoing program improvement and adjustment.

Third, it is inappropriate to rely on just one level of evaluation in order to make judgments about how well the program innovation is working. It is important to tap indicators at all levels, including levels three and four.

Fourth, it is important to focus first on formative evaluation using the framework, that is, on checking that the program is actually working well in practice (levels one to three) before making summative judgments about its impact (level four).

Fifth, expect to find that people in different roles may well give emphasis to indicators at different levels of evaluation. This is because performance in different roles in education is often judged using different indicators.

For example:

- *Politicians and senior administrators* may give priority to indicators at level one. They might focus on the quality of the documentation, how well it aligns with relevant policy documents. They may show interest in how much positive publicity a learning program gets or whether senior people in other educational sectors have heard of it and think it is 'good'. They might also be drawn to the efficiency indicators in level two (for instance, they might want to check the number of people enrolled, retention rates and how much the program is costing per learner).

- *Teachers and lecturers* may focus more on level three—on how the participating learners are reacting to their delivery of learning segments. They may also look to the quality of learner performance (level four) or to indicators like whether learners are turning up early and leaving late in order to gauge their enthusiasm for what is happening (levels two and three). In many cases the educators involved in a learning program innovation also look at the impact it is having not just on learners but on their own situation—time, career prospects, job satisfaction, pay rates and so on.

- *Learners* tend to be more interested in whether or not the program is delivering the improvements in their knowledge, skill, way of thinking or stance that they anticipated. That is, they will focus very much on level four indicators. For example, they may well look to indicators like whether their quality of life has improved, whether employment opportunities have been enhanced, whether they have developed the skills and knowledge they sought and so on. Learners may also look to how enjoyable and well taught each learning session is (level three).

It is vitally important that educators, administrators, employers, unions and other players recognise the existence of this wide diversity of indicators as they both develop and evaluate programs. They need to specifically determine if every preferred indicator can be catered for and, if not, how to reconcile them.

Sixth, individual assumptions about what distinguishes the most 'worthwhile' focus for a learning program also help determine which indicators different players emphasise.

One way to illustrate this point is to conceive of five 'tribes' in education, each with its own preferred set of goals for the exercise, its own distinctive preferences concerning a learning program's aims, focus, content, ways of relating to students and approaches to teaching and learning. This notion is represented in Table 2.2.

Each 'tribe' will most likely have quite different indicators for judging whether a learning program innovation was 'succeeding'. For instance, the 'traditionalist' might want to make sure that learners reproduce in tests and exams the valued information they impart. 'Self-actualisers' might be more interested in indicators that show that learners are happy, have raised self-esteem, and may eschew the idea of formal tests. 'Progressives' might look for evidence that priority problems identified by learners have been solved. 'Guerillas' might focus upon evidence of changed power structures and relationships and the increased 'empowerment' of participants, whereas 'organisational maintainers' might turn to indicators that demonstrate management satisfaction and productivity increases.

It should be emphasised, of course, that the attempt to split the whole educational enterprise into these five discrete tribes is quite artificial. In reality people often feel comfortable with the goals and indicators of more than one tribe. In fact it can be argued that there is a time and place for the focus of every tribe. The purpose of Table 2.2, therefore, is simply to point out that different assumptions about the goals of education will inevitably reveal themselves in the emphasis on different indicators for the 'success' of educational change efforts.

Table 2.2   The five 'tribes' of education: 'success indicators' and assessment preferences

Tribe	Goal/ success indicators	Focus	Content	Relationship with students/ trainees	Assessment preferences
Traditionalist	Disciplined minds Successful acquisition of traditionally 'worthwhile' knowledge, skills and attitudes	The individual	'Classics'—perennially valuable knowledge	Teacher superior to student/ trainee	Exam, essay, viva, multiple choice test, observation of performance, practical test
Self-actualisers	Achievement of full personal happiness 'Self-actualisation'	The individual	Feelings, personal experience Hidden assumptions to be surfaced and critiqued	Teacher facilitator to student/ trainee	Observation of body language, self-report techniques
Progressives	Increased ability of all individuals but especially the 'disadvantaged' to solve practical, 'real life' problems for the long-term benefit of society To reorder the 'queue' of the unemployed	Individual in a social context	Immediate problems and life needs of the student, especially survival problems	Teacher and student/ trainee equals	Real life evidence that an identified problem has been solved to the client's satisfaction
Guerillas	Creation of a new and better social order	Individual in a struggle to transform societal structures and priorities	Sources of oppression	Teacher and student/ trainee equals	Evidence of change in structures and relationships and learner reports that they feel more empowered
Organisational maintainers	Better organisational effectiveness (e.g. productivity and profitability) through successful training of members in skills, knowledge and attitudes required by the organisation	Organisation's needs	Determined by organisational needs assessment and broken down into specific behavioural objectives and performance indicators	Teacher superior to student/ trainee	Management satisfaction with delivery. Increased productivity

Sources: Darkenwald and Merriam (1982: 35–69); Hunt (1987: 78–81)

Take into account the informal and micropolitical side of program evaluation

Consider the following observation made by an experienced course coordinator:

> Anyone who thinks that all the really important decisions get made in formal open meetings is naive to say the least. Decisions about what is worthwhile, what should be pursued, what to abandon and so on get made in other far more informal, subtle ways. It's all about the interests of different groups, their assumptions about what is worthwhile and their comparative influence and jockeying to have their view prevail.

If what this program coordinator says aligns with your experience, it is clearly important to develop an ability to identify the many informal ways in which evaluation and micropolitics can influence what happens as learning programs are developed and implemented. It implies, also, that, if any program change process is to succeed, it is necessary to figure out how best to become involved in and navigate the micropolitical networks and situations in which informal evaluation occurs.

Informal evaluation is everywhere and drives what happens in every aspect of our lives. Consider, for instance, why we decide to go to one holiday destination and not another, why we pick this television program to watch and not that one, how we decide to discipline the kids, what causes us to feel happy or sad. In every case we are making a judgment about a situation and, on the basis of this, acting on our conclusions.

In exactly the same fashion, evaluation permeates the whole programming process in education. It is, as emphasised in Chapter 1, the driving force behind it.

This informal side of evaluation operates in a wide range of micropolitical contexts in education. It involves people using networks, power and influence to get things to turn out in ways that they think are *valuable*. So micropolitical strategies are actions intimately tied up with value judgments and the evaluation of events as they unfold. It is quite naive, as the program coordinator above observes, to think that decisions about what should change in education (or elsewhere) or how this might best happen occur primarily in formally constituted meetings. Typically, the key decisions have been arrived at long before this. The tendency for different subgroups with different 'tribal' loyalties to pursue their own agenda is always a possibility and needs to be taken into account as the change process unfolds.

Hoyle (1986) and Ball (1987) give a good introduction to the micropolitics of change in education. Their findings were confirmed in higher education in a research project in 1990 (Scott, 1990). A wide range of micropolitical strategies which different interest groups may resort to when educational change is in the air have been identified in such research. People of all 'tribal' persuasions are likely to use these tactics. Using them can be seen to be justifiable or reprehensible depending on whether the individual is part of the group whose dearest principles or self-interests are being threatened. The issue of whether the (micropolitical) means justify the (educational) ends is, itself, a value judgment. Micropolitical strategies that could be used by different interest groups in education include:[6]

- *Those used in informal contexts* Rumour, gossip, 'nobbling' people before meetings, rehearsing strategies before meetings, corridor 'caucusing', lobbying and use of informal influence, opposition, informal bargaining and striking deals.
- *Those used in more formal contexts* 'Displacement', negotiation, 'controlling talk', use of outside/higher authority, 'interpreting' consensus, 'pseudo-participation'.
- *Those used in both contexts* Calls for loyalty, 'debunking and stigmatising', humour and ridicule, non-verbal tactics, 'baronial politics', 'contrastive rhetoric and extremist talk'.
- *Strategic actions* 'Divide and rule', cooptation, exclusion, blocking (ideas and people), control of information flow, 'losing' recommendations, reference of matter to a subcommittee, 'rigging' agenda, 'massaging' the minutes.

The broader conception of 'evaluation' outlined above more accurately fits the daily reality of life in education than a conception which simply equates 'evaluation' with a formal test, an assessment task or a course evaluation questionnaire ('happy sheet') given out during or at the end of a learning program. Being able to work with the micropolitics of change and ongoing informal evaluation is, clearly, an essential change management skill.

Develop a comprehensive, feasible and clear program evaluation plan

The idea of seeing evaluation as occurring at these four levels, and as requiring the use of a variety of indicators, sources of data and informal as well as formal methods for gathering it will ensure that a comprehensive approach to evaluation planning is undertaken. The fact that evaluation occurs at every phase of the programming process and that specific people need to be given responsibility for different evaluation tasks should also be taken into account.

An example of how this might be done is presented in Table 2.3 where a comprehensive approach to the evaluation of an innovation in workplace basic education is outlined. The framework suggested in this table shows how different evaluation criteria can be tested using different sources of evidence and methods for gathering data at different phases of the program change process. It allows for the use of informal (i) as well as formal (f) data gathering methods and ensures that it is clear who is responsible for each evaluation task and when this task should be completed.[7]

This planning framework can be adapted for use in evaluating any learning program innovation. It should be emphasised that what is outlined in Table 2.3 is particularly comprehensive and everything suggested may not always be feasible. However, by using it as a starting point when discussing plans with others (especially senior administrators, funding bodies and colleagues), it will assist in identifying what aspects must be given emphasis and, most importantly, what ones are to be intentionally left out.

When using the tactics suggested in the table to make

Table 2.3   Workplace basic education evaluation plan

Phase	Evaluation criteria	Source of evidence	Method to gather data	Person(s) responsible	Results due
Upfront (before it starts)	Is the program seen as desirable? Which aspects are distinctive? Is the program feasible? Is there a shared and clear vision of what will happen?	Staff, CEOs, unions, teachers and students, relevant community and professional groups, strategic plans	Interview (i/f), survey, document analysis, structured group discussion	Program coordinator, Workplace Training Team (WTT)	15 Feb
	Level 1: Is the paperwork clear, logical, coherent, theoretically sound?	Staff, students, CEOs, relevant external bodies, educational 'experts'	Interview (i/f), document analysis, individual review	WTT	28 Feb
During implementation (once it is underway)	*Level 2:* Are human and material resources in place? General cost (efficiency) of program okay? Are enrolment numbers remaining okay?	Staff/resource section, invoices	Interview (i), document analysis	Program coordinator, WTT, resource manager	Ongoing
	Level 3: How effective are program structure, content, delivery, staff, assessment methods, timing, learning resources, location?	Staff, students	Observation, interview (i/f) and course satisfaction questionnaire	Program coordinator	Ongoing
	Level 4: Is there a 'positive' impact on:			Course lecturer	End of course
	(a) students' performance skills, way of thinking, stance, career, loyalty to the company, ability to self direct their learning?	Students, employers	Self report questionnaire, formal and informal assessment (on and off the job)	Program coordinator, WTT	Ongoing
	(b) staff performance skills and career?	Staff, students	Observation, self report and questionnaire, staff records	Program coordinator, WTT	Ongoing

Table 2.3 cont.

Phase	Evaluation criteria	Source of evidence	Method to gather data	Person(s) responsible	Results due
	(c) company's training; agency's productivity, visibility, competitiveness, level of support for training?	CEOs, public relations people, accountants	Interview (i/f), analysis of accounts, media reports, benchmark data	Program coordinator, CEO, WTT	Ongoing
	(d) external bodies' support for the program/company, levels of promotion of training, accreditation?	Relevant government, industry, union and educational bodies	Networking, interview, analysis of policy documents	WTT, program coordinator, CEO	Ongoing
	(e) extent of use of the work-based basic education program by other companies/groups?	Relevant companies, groups	Survey, analysis of media reports, networking	WTT, government coordinating agency	After pilot phase is over
Continuation (after it has been going for a while)	Does the program continue to be:				
	(a) part of normal company resourcing and staffing policies?	Relevant resource committee reports	Document analysis	WTT	Prior to end of pilot, then ongoing
	(b) built into the relevant industrial awards?	Awards	Document analysis	WTT	Near end of pilot
	(c) seen as relevant and desirable by key players or does it need adjustment?	Relevant government, industry and educational bodies	Networking, survey	Program coordinator	Ongoing
	(d) actively praised by past students with potential students?	Potential students	Networking, survey	WTT	Ongoing
	(e) staffed with competent people?	Staffing documents	Document analysis	WTT	Ongoing

Notes: i = informal, f = formal, WTT = Workplace Training Team

© G. Scott

judgments about how 'successful' a particular learning program change has been, a very important condition should be kept in mind, that is, any judgments made are *time specific*. For example, if the program is found to be working successfully at point x in time, this does not necessarily mean that this will be the case at some later point. This is because the context in which any education program operates is constantly changing. (Think, for instance, of the effect if the educator who delivered the program successfully for a number of years leaves and is replaced by a teacher quite unfamiliar with it.)

Work out how best to handle the most common program evaluation dilemmas

As evaluation decisions are made some of the more common dilemmas faced include how best to balance:

- rigour of assessment with relevance;
- the amount of credence that should be given to different players' success indicators;
- efficiency with effectiveness;
- a focus on assessing lower versus higher order outcomes (see Glossary);
- funding and time available with thoroughness of evaluation and assessment.

Probably the most common dilemma involves how to balance rigour (reliability) with relevance (validity) in assessment. For instance, it is a lot easier, cheaper and more reliable to study the paper work of a change or to look at efficiency indicators than it is to try to establish reliably if the change is working well and having the desired impact. Yet if we don't look carefully at the latter two features of evaluation, any judgments we make may very well be invalid (that is, irrelevant or insignificant).

Exactly the same dilemma exists when people use rigorous tests of lower order skills to indicate that the impact of the program on students has been 'worthwhile'. The performance of such skills (for example, the ability to perform set procedures, in a set order, to a set standard or to accurately regurgitate dictated information) is not what distinguishes a competent performer in work or life. What distinguishes competent performers (Scott, 1997) is their possession of higher order attributes like the ability to think flexibly and pro-actively, the ability to win over groups of people, the ability to get to the core of a problem quickly, the ability to tolerate ambiguity, learn from errors, take sensible risks and so on. Such attributes are highly relevant to what is now being expected of educational programs but they are excessively difficult to measure rigorously, reliably and cost-effectively.

A final evaluation dilemma concerns how best to ensure that relevant staff act on any negative feedback received during evaluation. Resolving this dilemma is very much tied up with the unique morale and culture of each workplace (see Chapter 3). If, for instance, staff are rewarded for identifying and working collectively on problem areas, then it is more likely that negative feedback generated through program evaluation will be acted upon. If, on the other hand, there is a climate of defensiveness and disaffection it will not. How well such dilemmas are resolved will, in part, influence how 'effective' each programming effort turns out to be.

Take the situation outlined in the Austec case study (see pp. 47–8) and assume that your suggested start-up strategies have been effective and that implementation is underway. Consider, with reference to the checkpoints given in this chapter and other relevant resources, what you would do if you were Austec's training manager to ensure that the *evaluation and monitoring* of this innovation are efficient and effective and will optimise the chances of its continuation. Consider who you would involve and how, what you would do and what factors and conditions you would give particular attention to.

CONCLUSION

The length of this chapter gives some indication of the complexity of the program change process in education. The chapter demonstrates the way in which program start up, design, implementation and evaluation are not discrete processes but are intimately connected, that is, what happens in one phase influences and is influenced by what happens in the others.

One of the problems with the process of program improvement and innovation in education is that, although good practice research on its management has been available for some time, practitioners have been either unaware of this or unsure of how to put it into practice. For this reason this chapter has gone to considerable lengths to provide practical insights, based on what we have learned from successful innovators, on how best to manage each phase of learning program change. The practical change management checkpoints which have emerged from this analysis should always be addressed if successful program change is to be achieved. This does not mean, of course, that they should be blindly followed (the silver bullet myth), only that they should be considered in terms of how they might apply in each unique situation encountered.

A number of recurring themes integrate what has been explored. They include: the importance of working collaboratively in small teams composed of those staff best positioned to make well informed and sound decisions concerning what should happen; the necessity of consulting with the people upon whom the change will have an impact early on in the process; and the importance of continually testing the quality of what is emerging by determining that it is relevant, desirable, clear and feasible.

Just as the various phases of the program change process in education are intertwined, so too are learning program and institutional change. Although being able to appropriately apply the program change strategies discussed in Chapter 2 is clearly a vital component of the change process in education, it is by no means all that is necessary. If the organisational and local workplace in which people attempt to apply such skills and knowledge is unsupportive, then even the best conceived learning program innovations will founder. In fact, one of the errors of early program innovation studies in education was to ignore the impact of the workplace context and the ways in which this might have to change in order to better accommodate the teaching and learning innovations that were being undertaken. It is to this other key, contextual, component of effective change management that we now turn.

3

MANAGING WORKPLACE IMPROVEMENT IN EDUCATION

*That our social environments influence our behaviour
is hardly arguable, and it makes good sense to try
to create productive environments for teachers . . .
there has been enough exploratory work to develop
strategies that have a reasonable probability for success.*

B. Joyce (1990)

In the past decade it has become increasingly clear that both the local workplace and the organisation of which it is part play a key role in determining how effectively learning programs actually pan out in practice. It is now recognised that it is no longer good enough just to give individuals all the knowledge and skills necessary to ensure that relevant, well designed learning programs are consistently designed and delivered unless equivalent attention is given to ensuring that the milieu in which these individuals are to operate is supportive.

We know, for instance, that even the best conceived learning program changes can soon falter if:

- the workplace is bogged down in useless paperwork and 'administrivia';
- the unit responsible for the learning program has an inappropriate management structure;

- the employing body has poor staff selection, promotion and support practices;
- the organisation fails to note excellence and reward it;
- planning procedures are unfocused, time consuming and unrelated to the unit's 'core business' which, in an educational service, is the consistent delivery of high quality learning programs;
- there are no quality enhancement, monitoring and review mechanisms in place;
- the workplace is characterised by anomie, alienation and backbiting.

This chapter poses the question 'How well does your educational workplace and the organisation of which it is part ensure that its administration, structure, staffing practices, planning tactics, quality assurance procedures and culture all work together to support the consistent delivery of high quality learning program innovations?'

Whereas Chapter 2 concentrates on 'good practice' in learning program development, implementation and evaluation, Chapter 3 concentrates on 'good practice' in organisational design and workplace relations. Whereas Chapter 2 looks at how best to ensure that learning programs succeed, Chapter 3 looks at what sort of organisation will best support this process. Whereas Chapter 2 is about educational change, Chapter 3 is about organisational change.

By comparing your workplace milieu with the research on 'good practice' and the standards outlined below, you should be able to identify aspects that match up well and others which warrant development. If aspects of a workplace's administration or operation which warrant enhancement are discovered then, in order to improve them, the same sorts of start up, implementation and evaluation tactics as those advocated in Chapter 2 will need to be adopted. The focus will simply have to shift from learning program innovation and enhancement to organisational innovation and enhancement.

Individuals' capacity to influence such developments will depend on their position in the organisation. If they are junior, all they might be able to do is to label a poor administrative or management tactic, using the 'good practice' research in the sections that follow to justify their point. If they are in a more senior management position, they will be better placed to actively initiate needed administrative, structural or procedural reform.

KEY CONCEPTS AND TERMS

An education service which actively and efficiently supports the development and delivery of consistently successful learning programs and is constantly seeking to enhance its operation can be said to be a 'quality' service. The term 'quality' is being used widely now in discussions of successful public and private sector performance. Terms like 'quality control', 'quality assurance', 'total quality management', 're-engineering', 'strategic networking', 'benchmarking', 'studies of best practice', 'continuous quality improvement and innovation' and 'quality review' are all part of the current lexicon. What exactly do these concepts mean and how applicable are the ideas that lie behind them to enhancing the operation of an educational service?

Quality

In everyday parlance 'quality' is used to refer to the intrinsic attributes and worth of a service or product. In particular, it refers to something which is 'high grade', something which is characterised by 'excellence'. For instance, we say 'That's a quality car' or 'That was quality food'.

However, as Cuttance (1995: 12) points out, leaders of the quality movement in industry and commerce like Feigenbaum, Deming and Juran use a somewhat different definition. They focus not on intrinsic excellence but on a market-driven definition of quality. They do this by building into their definition customer or user expectations. They refer to quality in terms of its suitability to a particular market, conformance to requirements, fitness for use or as something that meets the needs and pocket of the customer. This definition is implicit in observations like 'My car is good value for money' or 'For the money, that's just what I need'. So, when used in commerce and industry, the term quality often refers not to intrinsic excellence but to 'fitness for purpose', to the maximum standard that can be achieved, given the resources available and the demands of the market.

In the context of education it is probably best to combine the two definitions and give the whole notion some additional twists. For educators, quality should clearly be about the intrinsic merit of the learning programs being delivered (that is, their desirability and distinctiveness). But quality should also be about the fitness for purpose of what happens (that is, their relevance to employer and student demand and their feasibility). In addition, the quality of impact which such programs are having on learners (for example, the extent to which they add value to their capabilities) must be monitored. This requires the establishment of an agreed set of tracking measures with which to monitor performance as well as the entrenchment of mechanisms to ensure that any areas for enhancement identified are promptly and wisely addressed.

The fitness for purpose of the organisational infrastructure which supports such activities (that is, the relevance and efficiency of the education service's planning processes, administrative systems, support services, staffing systems etc.) must be concurrently monitored and any areas for enhancement identified there promptly addressed. So, when seeking to assess the quality of an education service, it is important that two interconnected aspects are addressed:

- The quality of the service overall, for example, the quality of its structure and general way of operating, the quality of its planning approaches, of its administration, overall monitoring processes, staff selection and support procedures and so on.
- The quality of what it produces as a result of all these activities, that is, the quality and impact of its core activities

81

like learning programs, and in some sectors, research, consultancy and community service.

Different approaches to quality

Many different approaches to quality management have been advocated over the past half-century, primarily in commercial and industrial settings. Some of the main variants of relevance to education are briefly reviewed below. The discussions by Cuttance (1995) and Peterson et al. (1997) are useful references in this regard.

Quality control

This was one of the earliest approaches to quality management. In it the quality of the outputs from a process are inspected in order to ensure conformity to pre-set standards. Poor products are discarded and non-conforming production processes are brought back into line. Such an approach may work well in some manufacturing contexts and might have limited applicability in education if 'products' are seen as being courses. It would not apply, however, if the 'product' is seen as being students.

This approach tends to be 'outside–in' and concentrates on experts determining what should happen, what standards are to be met and ensuring compliance with these requirements. There is little active involvement of local players in evaluating or reshaping what happens.

Quality assurance

Quality assurance (QA) is related to quality control but has more direct applicability to education. Quality assurance aims to assure identified customers and stakeholders that the appropriate policies, processes, structures and procedures are in place to guarantee that the design and delivery of core activities is of a consistently high standard.

Course development and review procedures are one example of a QA system in education. In order to make this process more formative, institutions can provide course teams with a set of quality guidelines and tests against which they can assess and enhance their design ideas. In some cases new course development teams are being linked with previously successful design groups. Consistent with what was advocated in Chapter 2, the intention of such developments is to make QA a collaborative effort and to avoid the tendency for course review committees to sit in isolated judgment on finalised proposals.

Total quality management

In total quality management (TQM) the emphasis shifts away from quality assurance towards continuous quality improvement (CQI). It is characterised by greater staff involvement and a more 'customer-oriented' focus. The idea is that, if there is constant monitoring of processes and the level of customer satisfaction with services and products and if any shortcomings identified are rectified quickly, the organisation will be better positioned to compete successfully in the market.

Total quality management, therefore, has an essentially inward and current focus. It concentrates predominantly on incremental change and the continuous improvement of existing provision. Examples in education include:

- The various mechanisms used to monitor the quality of course implementation and service delivery (for example, student satisfaction surveys, focus group research, student and employer advisory committees).
- The different ways some schools, colleges, training units or universities ensure identified areas for enhancement are wisely addressed (for example, the use of cross-functional action teams, task forces, working parties and so on).

Total quality management does not usually generate the radical breakthroughs or changes of direction that may be required in a highly competitive market. 'Reengineering', 'strategic networking' and 'benchmarking' have been advocated as ways to redress the essentially inward, evolutionary and current focus of TQM.

Reengineering

In the early 1990s Hammer and Champy (1993) advocated 'reengineering' as a mechanism to deliver the radical changes in the corporate sector which TQM could not. They argued that involving staff in identifying solutions when a dramatic change of direction was necessary would preclude serious consideration of certain potentially relevant options, like 'downsizing' or closing down operational units, because these were inimical to staff self-interest.

> In reengineering . . . SWAT teams of top managers and outside consultants descend on a process; take it apart; try to wring steps, time and costs out of it; and put in place a new plan of work (often involving information technologies) . . . For a variety of reasons 70% of such interventions fail: the 'outsiders' never understood the work well enough, technology wasn't the whole answer, the costs in employee morale outweighed the gains . . . In 1995, Champy renounced the earlier book's emphasis on 'heavy blasting', arguing that authentic gains in performance could only come from people within. (Marchese, 1997: 509)

In education, the recent system restructures in school and post-secondary education are an example of reengineering.

Strategic networking, benchmarking and studies of best practice

Strategic networking and benchmarking are preferable mechanisms to reengineering when radical change in educational organisations is deemed necessary. In strategic networking key local and overseas education institutions, along with those professional, business and community groups who are well placed to identify new, viable directions, are identified and a wide range of contacts are established. Forms of contact can include targeted study tours, exchanges and professional experience programs.

In benchmarking, equivalent enterprises which are performing better on shared development priorities are identified and workplace research is undertaken to establish how they achieved this. It is in this way that 'benchmarking' overlaps with 'best practice' research. A good example is the recent development of collaborative networks of universities (for example, the Australian Technology Universities' Network). One of the problems with benchmarking is that, in the private sector, where competition for profits is paramount, there is little incentive, if an organisation is the best performer in its class, to give equivalent operations elsewhere access to the secrets of its success. In the public sector, especially in education, one might assume that this would be less of a problem. However, recent changes in government funding policies and system restructures have created a far more competitive environment which is limiting the open sharing of strategies deemed to be 'commercial in confidence'.

Continuous quality improvement and innovation

This concept builds on the improvement notions of TQM and CQI but, like reengineering, strategic networking, benchmarking and best practice research, it gives explicit recognition to the fact that there will be times when a purely inward and incremental approach to change may not be enough. At such times an education service's capacity for innovation, for taking a quite fresh direction, will be necessary.

The concept of continuous quality improvement and innovation (CQII) acknowledges that continuous change in the operating context of organisations requires them to undertake continuous improvement or innovation in both their core activities and the administrative and support services which underpin them if they are to remain relevant and competitive.

In the search for solutions to CQII priorities, strategic networking and 'benchmarking' as well as the systematic use of internal experience through TQM can be used. Both an inward and an outward focus is therefore encouraged by CQII. It is CQII which, when supported by QA, is the recommended emphasis for quality management in education.

Quality review

In recent years both internal and external quality reviews have become popular in all sectors of education. Quality reviews usually examine every aspect of a particular institution not just its parts. It is likely that, when such reviews are undertaken in the future, they will focus not just on QA but on determining how well an educational service is positioned to engage in CQII.

The need for an approach uniquely suited to education

Extreme caution should be exercised in adopting any quality process exactly as it is used in industry or commerce, for reasons such as the following:

- Education is primarily a public sector not a private sector affair.
- What it aims to do is to add value to people's capabilities, not to deliver products of uniform or consistent quality.
- It is funded, at least in part, by governments and governments do not operate in the same way as the private sector. For example, businesses are driven by the profit motive, governments are motivated by the desire to get re-elected. Business can often take a longer-term view, governments typically set their horizon at the next election.

What might an approach which builds on relevant aspects of the above discussion look like if it were to be made uniquely relevant to an education service? It is around this question that the rest of this chapter turns.

DISTINCTIVE ATTRIBUTES OF EDUCATIONAL ENTERPRISES WHICH SUPPORT CONTINUOUS QUALITY IMPROVEMENT AND INNOVATION

Consider what this teacher says about her experience of different education settings: 'I've worked in both good places and bad places. The good ones brought out the best I had to offer, the bad ones turned off my enthusiasm completely.' These comments reflect something we have all experienced. Having a high level of personal competence is of no use unless the place in which we work—its culture, climate, way of operating—enthuses and encourages us to 'give of our best'. For this reason alone it is important to work out exactly what it is that characterises workplaces that bring out the best performance in people and to avoid the things that lead to staff alienation. As noted in Chapter 1, motivation is a core factor in effective change management.

There are other reasons as well. As the research on the change process reviewed in Chapter 1 and the discussion of the 'education programming swamp' in Chapter 2 suggest, the educator's world:

- is constantly changing and shifting;
- often leaves the educator to work, cope with change and struggle with difficulties in isolation;
- is always uncertain and somewhat unpredictable;
- is excessively value-laden and subjective;
- involves a mixture of individual action (acting on things amenable to individual influence) and drift (trying to cope with factors beyond individual control);
- requires an ability to continuously 'read' the significance of an extremely complex and unique combination of influences, people and factors and consistently 'match' an appropriate course of action to it.

Because this is the context in which we all must operate, each educational organisation and unit needs to have the type of structure, staffing tactics, planning and decision-making approaches, communication mechanisms, culture and climate which, in combination, optimise the chances that it can keep up with the demand for continuous quality improvement and innovation. This, as Fullan (1993: 4) observes, implies the development of a quite new conceptualisation of the structure and operation of an education system:

The new problem of change . . . is what would it take to make the educational system a learning organisation—expert at dealing with change as a normal part of its work, not just in relation to the latest policy, but as a way of life.

There is also increasing pressure for public sector organisations to be more transparently accountable for all that they do. Quality reviews are now, as noted earlier, becoming a regular feature in many sectors of education.

The research on successful educational organisations is clear (Fullan, 1993; Wilson & Daviss, 1994). The ones which succeed don't just select and actively support individuals who are effective at managing personal change and improvement. They are structured, managed and operated in such a way that the overall organisation itself is focused on the effective management of continuous organisational change and improvement. In this way individual and organisational change, individual and organisational learning are inextricably linked.

The key attributes of a workplace which is well positioned to manage continuous innovation and enhancement in both its learning programs and its operating environment are identified and discussed below.

Culture and climate

The culture and climate of a workplace can dramatically influence the level of commitment and enthusiasm which staff have for engaging in and sticking with change. If staff enjoy going to work, if the accepted ways of doing things in the workplace (its culture) are supportive of individuals and if staff get on well and can work constructively together (the workplace climate) then they are more likely to manage the demands on ongoing change effectively.

Workplaces characterised by backbiting, secretiveness, backstabbing, a lack of openness and high levels of intolerance have the opposite effect. Fullan and Hargreaves (1991), in their review, identified a number of recurring problems in educational workplaces:

- People felt overloaded with meaningless 'busy work'.
- Many staff felt undervalued—it was not expected that managers should actively seek out and praise successful performance; it seemed to be accepted practice to neglect incompetence or to write off some staff as being 'beyond redemption'.
- A norm of individualism and isolation prevailed.
- People, when they did associate, tended to fall into subgroups and engage in 'group think' (the tendency for a subgroup to expect its members all to think the one way).
- There was a general norm of 'powerlessness'—with staff using talk like 'Why don't they' rather than talk like 'Why don't we'. This norm was reinforced in places where attempted previous reform projects had not been well managed and had failed.

Climate and culture penetrate all operating components of an educational workplace—its structure, system of rewards, planning processes, communication systems, staffing practices and so on. To directly overcome problems like those identified by Fullan and Hargreaves is, therefore, not easy. Yet there are examples of educational workplaces which have done so and are not, therefore, 'organisationally ill'. Such workplaces are characterised by a culture and climate with the following characteristics:

- A focus on collaborative rather than competitive work practices and relationships. Traditional norms of 'us' (the local workers) and 'them' (the bosses) are replaced by more collaborative ones.
- An explicit attempt to identify and reward successful practice and collaboration (by acknowledging it in public forums and by incorporating it in promotion criteria).
- A willingness to take sensible risks and express dissent. This requires norms of trust, mutuality and reciprocity (Cox, 1995: 29).
- Leaders who actively model ethical and open ways of behaving.

- Identification and discouragement of backbiting, blame, rumour and micropolitics.
- Early public clarification of the facts surrounding key reforms by senior staff in order to put an end to unproductive gossip and rumour.
- Clear communication at the outset of any initiative as to the unnegotiable parameters within which it must operate.
- Widespread acceptance that ongoing change and improvement are inevitable, that continuous 'renewal' is the 'name of the game' and that everyone has a role to play in achieving this.
- Staff and learners are seen as having to play an active role in the process of continuous improvement and not passive recipients of decisions handed down from 'on high'.
- A bureaucratic norm (where getting resources and publicity is a more important indicator of success than successful implementation and impact) is replaced by a problem-solving one (where there is a bias for action, where local experiment is rewarded, where admitting and learning from errors is valued).[1]

The collegial culture associated with the most effective educational workplaces merits additional exploration. Consider what the following two authors say about the issue:

> Other things being equal, schools and colleges characterised by the norms of collegiality and experimentation are much more likely to implement innovations successfully. (Little, 1982)

> [I]t may be that the individual is the wrong focus of our attention. Perhaps we should be looking more carefully at constellations of individuals, groups, families, work teams. My experience tells me that people suffer most in their lives from failed or failing relationships . . . or from the lack of relationships . . . It follows then that the best way to deal with individuals may be to improve their relationships. (Farson, 1996: 90–1)

In order to achieve a collegial culture such places have been found to actively take the following steps:

- The main blocks to collaboration are identified and dealt with. These blocks include 'groupthink'[2] 'balkanisation and micropolitics',[3] 'contrived collegiality'[4] and a reward system that actively rewards individual not group achievement.
- Exactly who controls decisions about the different components of learning programs is made explicit and widely known.
- All aspects of workplace operation are regularly reviewed to ensure that they reinforce collegiality.
- Staff selection and promotion criteria and practices are regularly reviewed to ensure that the specific attributes and way of thinking characteristic of collegial workers are being emphasised.

However, two words of caution should be raised here. First, it is quite inappropriate to move into an exclusively collegial environment where absolutely everything must be done and decided together. As Michael Fullan (1993: 34–5) emphasises, there is a good side to individualism and having time to be and work alone:

> The capacity to think and work independently is essential to educational reform . . . The freshest ideas often come from diversity and those marginal to the group . . . Groups are more vulnerable to faddism than individuals . . . Group suppression or self suppression of intuition and experiential knowledge is one of the major reasons why bandwaggons and ill-conceived innovations flourish.

Second, collegiality and collaboration are not the same as consensus. As noted in Chapter 1, it is a myth that consensus is essential for effective change. In fact requiring consensus can actually prevent necessary changes from proceeding. For example, 'group think' (Janis, 1972) can encourage the people engaged in it to become increasingly defensive about negative feedback, unwilling to consider ideas which do not align with their preconceptions and dismissive of dissenting voices. Yet taking such things into account is essential if substantial change is to be achieved.

Staff selection and support

Staff selection and promotion procedures are central to the development of an effective education service. Without managers who have the stance, way of thinking, skills and knowledge profiled in Chapter 5 and teaching staff with the profile of the effective teacher (Scott, 1995a, 1997) even the best structured, best resourced education service cannot produce 'quality' outcomes for clients.

There is ample evidence (Scott, 1990; Fullan, 1991) that a positive working climate can be destroyed with alarming speed by appointing or promoting someone who is defensive, devious, self-aggrandising, cynical, disaffected or unable to work in a climate of constant change. Given the high costs of inappropriate appointments, it is essential that each education service identifies and uses 'best practice' in selection and promotion processes. Such practices are explored by Scott (1997). However, few educational enterprises explicitly apply such findings.

Equally challenging (both industrially and ethically) is what to do with staff who are clearly no longer contributing actively to the work of an educational service. Systems of performance appraisal and enhancement for staff are now prevalent in education. It is important that they are well conceived and focus on formative as well as summative assessment of staff performance.

All effective educational enterprises explicitly support the development of their staff. As Fullan (1991: 319) concludes, staff development in educational enterprises is 'both a strategy for specific instructional change and a strategy for basic organisational change in the way teachers work and learn together'. Staff development can include support to participate in accredited courses, the establishment of 'buddy systems' including systems of professional development and review,[5] the establishment of short workshops in response to staff needs, the organisation of staff exchanges with other centres, the establishment of electronic learning networks[6] and so on.

As noted in Chapter 2, change-specific learning support is

a distinguishing characteristic of educational organisations which are effective at managing ongoing improvement and innovation. Support can be provided when change is on the agenda simply by being sensitive to the aspects of human motivation as outlined in Chapter 1. Fullan (1993: 25) points to the importance of change leaders being sensitive to the emotional impact of change on motivation:

> Under conditions of uncertainty, learning, anxiety, difficulties and fear of the unknown are *intrinsic* to all change processes, especially at the early stages. One can see why a risk taking mentality and climate are so critical. People will not venture into uncertainty unless they or others appreciate that difficulties are a natural part of any change scenario. And if people do not venture into uncertainty, no significant change will occur (. . . problems are our friends).

Leadership

Effective educational leaders know how best to shape culture, develop a positive working climate, communicate their service's mission and priorities, coordinate quality assurance and enhancement in learning programs and support and reward staff as they grapple with ongoing change. There is now an extensive literature on what constitutes effective leadership in education. This is explored in detail in Chapter 5.

Identification and dissemination of good practice

There is increasing evidence that the best educational enterprises actively seek to learn from others. This finding was noted in Chapter 2 when discussing effective start-up strategies for learning program innovations. But it applies equally well as a tactic for enhancing the process of improvement at the organisational level.

Effective educational operations actively seek out equivalent enterprises which have been demonstrably successful in producing successful learning programs. When they find such places they study how they are structured, their climate and culture, their staffing practices, how they plan and make decisions, their communication systems as well as how they tackle the programming function. They ask managers and staff how they succeed in getting each of these components working so well. Then they adapt what they have learned back at their own workplace.

Learning from those who have 'trod the path' is a powerful tool for organisational and educational improvement. As noted earlier, 'benchmarking' is a specialised version of this general approach. There is also evidence that the most effective educational enterprises actively identify, publicise and reward good practice from within. This is a key tactic not just for improving overall quality but for raising motivation, developing a positive climate and shaping a more collaborative culture.

In general, the most effective enterprises are 'learning organisations',[7] places committed to continuous quality improvement and innovation. They constantly monitor their own practices, seek out relevant areas for enhancement or innovation, undertake change projects based on these and explicitly identify and share what has been learned from the whole process. In Chapter 4 the strategies used by an effective 'learning organisation' are taken up in more detail when workplace action research is discussed. Field and Ford's 1995 book *Managing Organisational Learning* is an important resource in this area.

Communication systems

The nature, extent and quality of communication in an educational organisation play a central role in determining how successful its management of ongoing change will be. As Duck (1993: 110) concludes:

> Managing change means managing the conversation between the people leading the change effort and those who are expected to implement the new strategies, managing the organisational context in which change can occur and managing the emotional connections that are essential for any transformation.

94

Poorly conceived, time consuming and unfocused systems of communication are one of the major blocks to efficient change management in present-day organisations. Recent rapid developments in information technology have created a double-edged sword. On the one hand, it is now much easier to communicate, but on the other hand, this can lead to 'communication overload'. This refers to the tendency to use the speed and ease of the new technology to create and send increasing numbers of memos, faxes, voice mail and Email messages around the workplace, even if the reasons for sending them or what will be done with the responses generated are unclear. It is vital, if an education service is to go about its prime business of developing, delivering and enhancing learning programs, that staff don't become buried in useless information and calls on their time.

The best enterprises have directly addressed this problem and utilise the available technology sparingly and strategically. For instance, whenever a request for information is sent out, it is made quite clear why it is needed, how it will help support the service's core business and when the person sending the request will report back on exactly how the response was used. In some cases the person best situated to comment on a key issue is delegated the task of drafting a response and this is circulated for key players to simply identify what should be added, deleted or emphasised. This is clearly a far more efficient way to proceed than to ask everyone to write out what they want included at the outset and then attempt to compile their input.

In the last decade, as the need to involve staff and other players in decision making has been more recognised, the most popular involvement device has been to 'have a meeting'. In some places *the meeting* has become so prevalent that there seems little time to actually deliver learning programs. In many locations meetings are used as a form of what Andy Hargreaves calls 'contrived collegiality'. The most successful enterprises use meetings more judiciously and rely on intense ongoing informal communication (Peters & Waterman, 1984: 218ff) as the preferred tactic for involvement.

Large group meetings are often best used to launch a project, provide the facts of the matter, set the unnegotiable parameters for an initiative, to put an end to rumours, to check agreement with a final plan of action, to brief key players or to check they are clear on their different roles in an upcoming activity. They are less suited to the sort of ongoing informal communication necessary, for instance, to develop sound learning programs (see Chapter 2). Nor should meetings be used to gather in data which could be provided electronically from the desktop or by a memo.

Even when meetings are warranted they are typically poorly run. For instance, meetings need to be well chaired. Participants need to be clear on why they are there. Briefing papers should be sent out sufficiently in advance to allow adequate reading time and reflection. The chair needs to ensure that discussion is focused and action-oriented. Rambling contributions need to be cut short. At the end of the meeting the individuals who are to take action on any matters arising need to be identified and what they will do agreed upon.

If the reason for calling a meeting no longer applies, cancel it. Don't carry on with a meeting simply because it is in everyone's diary.

Another key communication task that is often poorly handled concerns *delegation*. Active involvement and a more collaborative approach to change management means that one person must not do all the work. This implies that the different tasks which make up a change project must be delegated. When this is undertaken it is vitally important that the manager delegating a task checks that the individual being asked to carry it out:

- has the interest and skills to undertake it;
- is clear on and in agreement with what is to be achieved;
- knows that the manager is available to assist should this be necessary;
- is clear on and agrees with the indicators that will be used to judge that the task has been successfully carried out.

The best approach to delegation is almost identical to that used when negotiating a learning contract (see Anderson et al., 1996). An excellent film on delegation and coaching is the John Cleese film, *The Helping Hand* (Video Arts, 1990).

A final important aspect of communication concerns the need for *documentation* of key policies and procedures. It should be emphasised, however, that it is a waste of time producing such documents if they are not 'owned' by the staff who are to use them. To ensure ownership, staff must help write them. This can be done by inviting staff in various roles to describe best practice in the area under consideration, to incorporate this in the resulting document and invite user review before it is finalised. If a small group of isolated senior staff produce a policy and procedures manual or a strategic plan, only they are likely to understand what is written in it and only they are likely to refer to it.

Administrative support

Effective educational organisations have figured out how best to align their administrative culture and procedures with their educational purpose. As emphasised in Chapter 1, administrative procedures should never become an end in themselves. They must always be seen as being a means to an end—the effective and efficient support of high quality learning outcomes for clients.

Consider what the Hon. Jim Hacker in the television series *Yes Minister* found when he visited St Edward's Hospital.

> Today I paid an official visit to St Edward's Hospital . . . I met Mrs Rogers, the Chief Administrator, and . . . was shown several empty wards, several administrative offices that were veritable hives of activity, and finally a huge deserted dusty operating theatre suite . . . I asked her if she was not horrified that the place was not in use.
>
> 'No,' she said cheerfully. 'Very good thing in some ways. Prolongs its life. Cuts down running costs.'
>
> 'But there are no patients,' I reminded her.

She agreed. 'Nonetheless,' she added, 'the essential work of the hospital has to go on.'

'I thought the patients were the essential work of the hospital.'

'Running an organisation of five hundred people is a big job, Minister,' said Mrs Rogers, beginning to sound impatient with me . . .

I told her that this situation could not continue. Either she got patients into the hospital, or I closed it . . .

Mrs Rogers was unshakeable in her self-righteousness. 'It is one of the best-run hospitals in the country,' she said. 'It's up for the Florence Nightingale award.'

I asked what that was, pray.

'It's won,' she told me proudly, 'by the most hygienic hospital in the Region.' (Lynn & Jay, 1984: 195–7)

Administrative staff can be a key source of support in the design and delivery of effective learning programs. But for them to give the right sort of support it is vitally important that they are clear on what the educational goals of the service are, that they understand and are committed to how they can help in achieving these and are valued for the contributions they make.

In ineffective educational workplaces administrative personnel are unclear on the connection between their work and the service's primary goal of consistently delivering successful learning programs. They rarely get to see the consequences of their activity for learners and receive little praise or appreciation for their efforts. As a consequence they either lose perspective completely or become alienated because they see no meaning in what they are doing. They start to talk about 'working to rule' and are often found to be benignly trying to make it as hard as possible for educators to get the resources they need or to move paperwork through the system efficiently. They show little interest in trying to alter or manipulate reporting systems in ways necessary to support the efficient implementation of learning program innovations or enhancements.

The idea, then, is to avoid the tendency for educational

workplaces to become 'loosely coupled' (Wieck, 1976). In 'loosely coupled' workplaces there is plenty of activity but what happens in one part of the system often contradicts what is being attempted in another. The aim, therefore, is to ensure that the structure of the workplace emphasises coherence, interconnection and focus without stifling local initiative.

Structure

Restructures of educational systems are increasingly common. However, the rationale for introducing one structure for decision making and distribution of resources over another is often hazy. Probably the most appropriate approach is to bring together seemingly paradoxical approaches which take into account, as Fullan (1993: 37) observes, that '[c]entralisation errs on the side of overcontrol, decentralisation errs towards chaos.'

A structure of power and decision making which balances top-down and bottom-up input into the development of learning programs and other educational initiatives has been found to be the one best suited not just for education (Fullan, 1991: 200–9) but also for other enterprises (Pascale, 1990; Binney & Williams, 1995; Handy, 1995). The best solution is to make explicit what the centre is best equipped and positioned to look after (for example, securing external resources, keeping an eye on upcoming policy changes in government, identifying and disseminating best practice, formulating mission) and what the local unit is best equipped and positioned to look after (the nuts and bolts of program development, quick responsive support for learning programs, ensuring effective monitoring and adjustment of programs and practices). The aim, therefore, is for the centre and the local units to *complement not duplicate* what each other does and to work together to meld what they learn. The flow of information is focused and is both bottom-up and top-down. The centre and local units, as Fullan (1993: 38) observes, must clearly see the need for each other. In a similar fashion the organisation's structure and reward system should ensure that what academic/teaching staff focus on and what administrative/support staff do is consistently linked and complementary.

If, as is now being widely advocated, there needs to be more responsibility given to people 'at the coalface' for particular functions, then parallel attention will have to be given to restructuring their work in order to allow them adequate time to carry out this additional work. It will require those who are at the centre of the organisational structure to be willing to give these powers away. It will require explicit attention to figuring out how best to give greater local autonomy without losing overall system coherence and continuity of purpose.

The ideal structure seeks to link various operating elements (administration, program development, resourcing and so on) efficiently and makes explicit who has final responsibility and accountability in each area and why. Those who have the power to take a decision need be clear that they are also responsible and accountable for what happens as a result of it. The rule should be 'No power without responsibility and accountability'.

The service's structure should facilitate adequate consultation with key interest groups. Consultation must not, however, be confused with power and responsibility. The former gives a player the right to give advice on a proposed course of action, but power is concerned with who, in the structure of relationships at the education service, is to be accountable for processing, making decisions about resourcing and acting on such advice.

The overall focus, as noted in the discussions of administration and communication above, is to come up with a structure that is explicit, coherent, linked, mutually reinforcing and which minimises 'busy work', 'paper shuffling' and time wasting. Such a structure actively encourages continuous enhancement of the service rather than institutionalising vested interests dedicated to the maintenance of the status quo at all costs.

Monitoring processes

The most effective workplaces not only seek to put in place the things advocated above, they specifically monitor their performance, always with a view towards their continuous improvement. This can be achieved by using both formal means (for example, staff satisfaction surveys and focus groups on how well various components of the service are currently working) and informal means (for example, the sort of unsolicited feedback that can arise if a positive staff climate has been achieved). Such places also monitor how well each of the components that make up their whole operation are working together. Some educational units have an informal 'ideas committee' through which ideas for organisational improvement are channelled.

The most effective educational services use data on the outcomes of their learning programs in a very specific way. They look for learning program components and learning outcomes that are not succeeding and, once these are identified, they look back to what the service might have been doing wrong that would explain this. They then seek to modify that aspect of the institution's operation to overcome the inadequacies identified.

Documentation and statistic keeping

All effectively operating education services have very efficient information-recording and retrieval systems. Documentation can be of existing policies, practices and procedures, of plans for improvement, of learning programs, evaluation plans, assessment records and of data which must be retained for legal reasons. Statistics on participation in various centre activities also need to be collected.

While collecting statistical data may appear to be a chore, statistics can be strategically useful. For example, demand, usage, graduation and employment rates can generate trend data with which to argue for increased resources. More general documentation like a policy and procedures manual may also be useful in any quality reviews to which the school, college or university may be subject or to assist in the induction of new staff.

Planning and decision making

Many approaches to planning and decision making fail to focus on making desired change happen or to support it. As John A. Lincoln is reported to have said, '[a] committee is a cul de sac to which ideas are lured and then quietly strangled'.

Cuttance (1995: 13) notes that, in the way in which they go about their planning and decision making, the best educational operations:

- have a client focus;
- have a clear direction and purpose;
- use the focused involvement of key players to develop informed decisions about what should happen;
- use carefully collected evidence to inform decision making;
- emphasise the interrelatedness of administrative, management and educational processes;
- have as their prime emphasis the ways in which student learning outcomes can be improved;
- focus on continuous improvement based on experience;
- track progress and assure outcomes are achieved.

Much of the discussion earlier in this chapter and in the preceding one is supportive of what Cuttance is saying.

Of particular interest in recent years has been the notion of 'strategic planning'. In his book, *The Rise and Fall of Strategic Planning*, the well known management analyst Mintzberg (1994) is critical of the tendency for strategic planning in many organisations to concentrate too much on the production of 'paperwork' like annual strategic plans which are not 'owned' by staff and which, once produced, are not referred to again. He calls for less emphasis on specialist 'planners' writing plans and for more active support of ongoing strategic *thinking* by everyone involved.

Some of Mintzberg's key points are that:

- Real change requires adaptive learning and this can only occur when thinking and action are integrated and ongoing.
- 'People act in order to think and think in order to act' (p. 286); formalised processes of strategic planning artificially separate thinking from action and operate under the false assumption that thinking must be complete before action.
- What is needed for successful performance as an organisation is strategic thinking in conjunction with strategic action, not strategic planning.
- Too much search for formalisation on paper is the main fallacy of most planning.
- 'Investing so much energy in concocting the future on paper and draining so much commitment from those who are supposed to act, means that necessary actions just don't get taken' (p. 213).
- Standardised planning reflects an obsession with control which, in turn, reflects a fear of uncertainty and of taking sensible risks.
- Centralised planning actually discourages the commitment it aims to engender.
- Rigid planning processes discourage the flexibility, action and creativity necessary for 'adaptive learning' (p. 173).
- The best approach is to develop an organisation in which as many people as possible are willing, able and encouraged to get involved in an ongoing process of 'adaptive learning' and strategic thinking and not to concentrate on the production of detailed annual plans which are to be rigidly adhered to; this process must involve both a top-down and a bottom-up approach; the general tactic should be to involve everyone in an ongoing cycle of reflection–action–reflection. The motto should be 'ready, fire, aim', not 'ready, aim, aim, aim'.

Another recently popular catchcry—the call for 'vision-driven' change—must be treated with the same caution as strategic planning. In both instances the problem is that, in the real world of education, real understanding of the possibilities and clarity of vision comes during implementation not before it. We don't know what exactly is the best way to do something until we try, review and refine it. Fullan (1993: 31–2), when drawing out the implications of this way of thinking for the effective management of educational change, concludes:

> 'Ready, fire, aim' is the more fruitful sequence if we want to take a linear snapshot of an organisation undergoing major reform. Ready is important, there has to be some notion of direction, but it is killing to bog down the process with vision, mission and strategic planning, before you know enough about dynamic reality. Fire is action and inquiry where skills, clarity and learning are fostered. Aim is crystallising new beliefs, formulating mission and vision statements and focussing strategic planning. Vision and strategic planning come later, if anything they come at step 3, not step 1.

How to put into practice what Mintzberg and Fullan are advocating is outlined in practical terms in Chapter 4 when the tactics of workplace action research in education are discussed.

In general, the best approach to planning and decision making in education brings together tactics which appear contradictory.[8] For example, as noted in Chapter 1, such an approach seeks to strike an appropriate balance between:

- top-down and bottom-up strategies;
- listening and leading;
- stability and change;
- optimising the quality of the service's learning programs and its milieu;
- enhancement and innovation;
- pan-institutional and unit-specific change;
- educational and administrative staff quality and support;
- looking inside and outside;
- planning and implementation;
- listening to resistors and enthusiasts.

Hope High case study

Hope High is an inner city high school catering for students from 30 different nationalities. In a workplace research project the following profile of the way the school operates and its prevailing culture and climate emerges.

1 Staff report working longer and longer hours and having to be involved in a wider range of activities than ever before. Considerable levels of stress and uncertainty are reported and a number of the staff interviewed report that they feel that their extra efforts are going unnoticed.

2 There appears to be little contact between different teaching departments and high levels of 'baronial politics' in which heads of department vie for their share of diminishing resources. Even within some departments there are different subgroups, each group typically making disparaging remarks about the other.

3 The principal is seen by the majority of staff as being well meaning, conscientious but lacking the ability, as one staff member put it, 'to grasp the nettle, and take the hard decisions'. When interviewed, the principal reports feeling totally isolated and unable to win the support of staff. He claims that his day is one of continuous crisis management and having to handle constant problems with staff, students, parents and head office. He reports feeling that everything is sheeted home to him.

4 There is an active Parents & Citizens Association. However, few of the school's non-English-speaking parents participate.

5 As more and more decision making and responsibility for continuous quality improvement (CQI) has been devolved to the school, the principal has

attempted to set up a series of 'change teams' to handle the many areas in which improvement is needed. In discussing the operation of these teams the following comments from staff were typical:

- 'All we ever seem to do now is meet. The same people dominate each meeting. Nothing is ever followed up and the meetings are allowed to drift on for hours.'

- 'It's fine to be given the responsibility to tackle things like our new reporting system but, quite frankly, we were all thrown in at the deep end. We had no resources to fall back on but our own experience. I really don't think we were very efficient or effective as a team. We just seemed to bumble along without direction or leadership.'

- 'The way I see it is that if something succeeds, head office, the boss or my head of department take all the credit. If it doesn't work we get all the blame.'

- 'We have these professional development days. But they are usually too general to be of any use.'

6 Communication is cited as a common problem. Comments like the following are typical:

- 'There's an endless stream of memos. You answer them but you never see the results.'

- 'It's meetings, meetings, meetings. I'm actually paid to teach, mark and prepare but every spare moment seems to be taken up with another meeting.'

- 'I wish I knew what the priorities for improvement were. It seems to be one thing this week and another the next. And where's the principal when you need him?'

7 It emerges that there is a small group of staff who are involved in just about everything, another group

which is conscientious but less active in areas beyond their own teaching and a small group who are called 'the slackers'. These are the people who have a reputation for actively avoiding work. Considerable levels of concern are expressed that 'the slackers' are never called to account.

8 The office staff, when interviewed, report feeling generally unappreciated, overworked and exploited.

Given the situation outlined in the case study and the research outlined above, identify:

1 in what ways the Hope High case is similar to or different from the current milieu of your workplace;
2 three or four initial strategies you would adopt if you were asked to enhance the milieu of Hope High.

CONCLUSION

It should now be clear why it was emphasised in Chapter 1 that program change and organisational change must go hand in hand. There are two main ways in which this happens.

First, just as every good learning strategy requires the support of a well developed and appropriate learning resource, so too every learning program development requires an operating context which provides the specific support necessary for it to function effectively. That is, depending on its scope, every learning program innovation will generate some need for change in the organisation's administration, resource distribution, staff support procedures and infrastructure.

Second, and more fundamentally, there is the need, given the continuously shifting environment in which education must operate, for each education service to explicitly develop its capability to manage continuous quality improvement and innovation (CQII) efficiently and effectively in *both* its core activity of teaching and learning and in the milieu intended to support it.

To enable readers to address these challenges, guidelines on how best to shape the key components of effective workplace operation in education have been provided and illustrated. It has been emphasised that all of the following workplace components should be considered: culture and climate; staff selection and support; leadership; identification and dissemination of good practice; communication systems; administrative support; structure; monitoring processes; documentation and statistic keeping; and approaches to planning and decision making.

The approach embodied in these guidelines directly addresses the aspects of motivation and the myths of effective change management identified in Chapter 1.

But how exactly can educators committed to enhancing the quality of their workplace and its capacity for CQII in learning programs in the ways suggested in Chapters 2 and 3 actually do this? It is around this question that the next chapter turns.

4

WORKPLACE RESEARCH FOR CONTINUOUS IMPROVEMENT AND INNOVATION

We rise to great heights by a winding staircase.

Sir Francis Bacon

In the previous chapters the importance of figuring out how best to set, shape and implement change priorities has been a recurring theme. For instance, it was argued in Chapter 2 that the quality of learning programs would be enhanced if, for each new learning program:

- during start up, change teams sought to identify and learn about what other educators had been doing in similar contexts to their own (best practice research) and if they interviewed key players in their own organisation to gather in their views on what might best happen;
- during implementation they sought to gather in evidence from a variety of sources to monitor and evaluate how well their program innovation or enhancement was panning out in practice.

In Chapter 3 the same sorts of strategies were advocated but this time with a focus on gathering in data about the quality of workplace functioning in general—its structure, operating procedures, climate, culture, planning tactics and so on, again with the view of continuously enhancing the performance of the education service concerned.

In order to operate effectively in these ways it is necessary to become skilled in the use of a particular type of research—a practical, action-focused approach called 'workplace action research'. Workplace action research and workplace learning are intimately related. It is through the former that the latter occurs. In this chapter such an approach is introduced and practice in using it is given.

If the majority of the staff in an educational workplace become skilled in the tactics of workplace action research and self-directed learning there is a firm foundation for building a 'learning organisation' (Field & Ford, 1995)—the primary requirement for an enterprise to thrive in today's constantly changing environment. It is in this way that individual and organisational change are so closely intertwined.

This chapter provides an overview of the spiral of workplace action research. It discusses its place in a broader set of research approaches as well as its underlying philosophies and outlines something of its history. Some guidelines for reporting and effectively disseminating the outcomes of an action research project are given and the skills of efficiently and effectively locating and reviewing relevant change research articles are discussed.

WORKPLACE ACTION RESEARCH COMPARED WITH OTHER APPROACHES TO RESEARCH

There is rapidly increasing interest in establishing that the large investment made in educational research and scholarship is paying dividends on the ground, especially in terms of demonstrably improving the quality of teaching and learning experienced by students. For example, the July 1998 issue of Australia's *Campus Review* reported that in the United Kingdom a study had been commissioned by the Department of Education and Employment to examine the direction, organisation, funding, quality and impact of educational research, and that a similar review of the field was being commissioned by the Australian Research Council.

Directly connected with this interest is the issue of determining what approaches to educational research are most likely to have a direct and positive impact on practice. As Fullan and Connelly (1987: 31) observed a decade ago:

> Scholarly research which meets the requirements for publication in refereed journals will add to the understanding of basic processes . . . but other kinds of research and writing are also valuable for informing practice. Indeed, good field-based research can generate better theories even when judged by the criteria of pure scholarship.

One way in which to get an overview of the range of research approaches possible is to extend the notion that there are different 'tribes' in teaching and learning (Chapter 2) to those in the area of educational research. Table 4.1 suggests that there are four 'research tribes', each with its own preferred research style and purpose. It is suggested that these research groupings vary in their distinguishing characteristics, origins, advantages and disadvantages, their preferred research metaphor and techniques.

As emphasised when discussing this notion in Chapter 2, it is not implied that individuals are ever solely committed to just one tribal perspective. Rather, every one of the perspectives outlined below has its place. The art is to work out when to adopt any particular one and when not to. In studying Table 4.1, consider how the focus and approach of workplace action research are particularly suited to supporting practical change management.

A SHORT HISTORY OF WORKPLACE ACTION RESEARCH

Of the four different approaches to educational research outlined in Table 4.1 the one which has shown itself to be most

Table 4.1   The research 'tribes' in social science and education

Tribe	Style of research and purpose	Main characteristics	Origins of the approach	Advantages and disadvantages	Preferred research metaphor and methods
Photographers	*Style:* Survey *Purpose:* To give an overall picture of people's attitudes, views, opinions or characteristics at a particular point in time	Careful attention to definition of population, sampling, question and survey design An outside-in view of research	The census methods first used in early 19th century	*Advantages:* Can give a quick and comparatively cheap overview of where people stand on a particular issue or overall population characteristics and the general dimensions of a problem *Disadvantages:* Open to bias or can miss vital factors because the survey questions don't tap them May be superficial in measuring sensitive or difficult aspects of behaviour	*Metaphor:* Snapshot *Methods:* Interview, questionnaire
Experimenters	*Style:* Controlled experiment *Purpose:* To specifically connect cause with effect by controlling for all extraneous and potentially contaminating influences	The establishment of strict experimental conditions The unbiased selection of an experimental and control group Application of one treatment to the experimental group and another to the control group Use of a reliable and valid set of empirical methods to measure and compare treatment effects Often involves a pre-test and a post-test An outside-in view of research	19th century Positivism as espoused by people like Auguste Comte	*Advantages:* Can help connect a specific cause with effect better than a survey or an ethnography *Disadvantages:* Hard to treat one group in one way and another in a different way in real life Causes of social phenomena are usually multiple and changing Hard to do experiments on politically or socially sensitive problems	*Metaphor:* Puppeteer or explorer *Methods:* The experimental method

Table 4.1 cont.

Tribe	Style of research and purpose	Main characteristics	Origins of the approach	Advantages and disadvantages	Preferred research metaphor and methods
Naturalists	*Style:* Ethnography *Purpose:* To reveal the complex patterns of customs, habits, and rituals of everyday life in a specific social group and setting	Involvement in natural, real-life situations in all their complexity Researcher takes a subservient role An inside–out view of research	Social and cultural anthropologists of the early 20th century	*Advantages:* Captures the spontaneous activity and complex reality of groups *Disadvantages:* Time consuming and laborious Problems of group acceptance and of researcher presence biasing behaviour Results may not be representative and it is hard to know what data are signficant and what are not.	*Metaphors:* Immersion and illumination *Methods:* Field work, case study, participant observation, ethnography
Activists	*Style:* Action research *Purpose:* Research that leads to change in practice and is based in a particular context	An on-the-spot and cyclical procedure to identify the nature of and deal with a concrete problem in a particular context It is change-oriented A back and forth view of research	Action research first used by Lewin and Chein, Cook and Harding in the 1940s and by Corey in the 1950s	*Advantages:* Links ongoing workplace change, learning and research Best suited when a specific knowledge is required for a specific problem in a specific situation *Disadvantages:* Requires considerable levels of collaboration, time and organisational support to work	*Metaphors:* Coalface activist, swamp negotiator, architect-builder, team member *Methods:* A wide variety of the above methods are potentially relevant as are document analysis, critical incident techniques and group processes Particular techniques are specifically selected on the basis of how they will most efficiently and effectively make sense of and achieve a practical solution to a particular priority problem in a particular context

Sources: J. Bell (ed.) (1984); Oja and Smulyan (1989)

directly connected to change in daily practice is action research. This, argues Hunt (1987: 109), is because:

> Unless theories come from practice, they will not apply to practice . . . When theorists are also practitioners, their theories are bound to be more relevant to practice because they necessarily take into account the practical context to which they apply.

Sharon Oja and Lisa Smulyan in their book *Collaborative Action Research* (1989) give a historical overview of this style of research.[1] They identify the following major developments from its origins in the US in the 1940s.

The 1940s

The US social psychologist Kurt Lewin (1948) first used the term 'action research' in the 1940s. He argued that, in the sphere of social science, 'research that produces nothing but books will not suffice'. His focus was on social action and much of his early post-World War II work concentrated on significant social problems like prejudice, authoritarianism and industrialisation. He directly attacked the exclusivity of social scientists arguing that, in order to understand and change social practice, social scientists had to include practitioners in all phases of the research process in order to discover relevant theory and link it directly to social action.[2]

Individuals like Chein, Cook and Harding (1948) reinforced Lewin's general perspective in the late 1940s when they emphasised that action researchers studied problems which grew out of the community rather than out of their own knowledge and worked to make discoveries which resulted in positive change in the community setting(s) under question. Here there is a clear emphasis on the importance of one of the hallmarks of action research—the close, two-way relationship between theory and practice, between investigation and practical change.

In the early 1950s Stephen Corey (1952) was amongst the first to use action research in the field of education in the US. He argued that the scientific, objective approach to research (for example, experimental or survey research) had never been of great utility for educators because the generalisations made could never be usefully connected to the unique and ever changing reality of daily practice. He emphasised a key assumption and adult learning principle—that educators (like most other practitioners) are more likely to change their practices (and thereby improve the quality of their students' learning) if they can learn how to study the consequences of their own teaching rather than hearing about what someone else has discovered. In other words, as adult learning theory and the review of motivation in Chapter 1 emphasise, people are only likely to change if they personally see a reason for doing so. In this way another popular term, often associated with action research, came into being—'grounded theory', that is, the idea that sound theory can be seen in the ways in which effective practitioners go about their work. This relationship is indicated in sayings like 'there is nothing as theoretical as good practice' and 'there is nothing as practical as a good theory' (Hunt, 1987).

The 1950s and 1960s

Between 1953 and 1957 the fledgling interest in action research in education declined. The universities hit back with accusations that action research was methodologically weak, that it was 'unscientific', and lacked 'rigour'. Academics withdrew to their university rooms to produce studies more acceptable to their colleagues. Research quality in education was measured more by where studies got published and less by what sort of impact they had on the nature and quality of day-to-day teaching and learning.

Those academics who led the attack against action research during this period asserted that:

- research has no place for the amateur;
- educators should put their time into teaching and they should not waste their time carrying out research which is of dubious quality anyway;
- action research is not 'real' science because it does not

meet the criteria associated with valid and reliable experimentation;

- workplace problem solving does not involve theory building or relate to a larger body of theory and knowledge and is, therefore, little more than quantified commonsense;
- action research needs a special sort of leadership and this is not available.

They predicted that most action research projects would, therefore, fail. This, they said, would have a deleterious effect on staff morale and doing nothing would be better than that. Such views are still held by many people and must be accounted for if action research is to be taken seriously, especially by policy makers.

The distinct split between science and practice which developed in the 1950s carried over into the 1960s. Research reports and writing became so densely packed with jargon that they were virtually indecipherable to the ordinary practitioner. Federal education agencies in the US between 1954 and 1972 reinforced the trend by inviting university scholars to apply for federal research funding, with little more accountability for the quality of the outcomes than the submission of a report. A positive impact on practice did not feature strongly as a success indicator. Any action research that was done in this period tended to be carried out under the direction of an 'expert' consultant. This procedure, for instance, was used in the Schools Council Humanities Curriculum Project in the UK in the late 1960s.

The 1970s and 1980s

Only after 1972 in the US, with the establishment of the National Institute of Education, was there again an attempt to encourage a more demonstrable link between educational research and practice. A parallel trend occurred in the UK and in Australia during the same period. For instance, in Australia it was after a Labor government came into power in 1972 that the Australian Schools' Commission, the State Innovations'

Councils, Education Centres and National Research and Development Centres in Education were established.

By the mid-1970s action research had experienced a resurgence of interest and the number of educators experimenting with it expanded. This trend was driven by growing researcher and user dissatisfaction with the results of traditional research approaches as well as by teacher dissatisfaction with traditional forms of staff development where outside 'experts' lectured practitioners on the results of their research. By the mid-1970s, the criticism that remote, 'outside–in' styles of research were of little practical use in the turbulent conditions in which educators had to operate gained stronger and stronger voice. 'Outside–in' research approaches and the prescriptive advice from the 'experts' who ran them became more frequently greeted by practitioners with incredulity, boredom or mockery. The following quip (quoted by Winter, 1989: 65) from the *Times Educational Supplement* in 1980 is typical: 'Research either tells you something you knew already, or tells you nothing, or tells you something which is obvious nonsense.'

It was increasingly argued that 'outside–in' models of research and development gave the implementers of the results (the teachers) no ownership or understanding of the research agenda and therefore gave them little incentive to adopt any of the changes recommended. By the late 1980s field-based, action-oriented research had become increasingly accepted as a legitimate and valuable form of research. As Hunt (1987: 1) puts it:

> Research-based proposals do not work in education because the knowledge is not 'out there' to be discovered by researchers but 'in here', in the heads, hearts and actions of experienced teachers. Proposals for educational change must, therefore, begin with the experienced knowledge, skilled performance and intuitive sensitivity of experienced practitioners: teacher as expert.

By now the connection between workplace action research and experiential learning had been made more explicit (Kolb, 1984; Schön, 1987; Fullan, 1990). This enabled practitioners and reformers in education to better see how workplace action research, learning and change could be more closely linked.

The present

It is now quite clear, as Chapters 2 and 3 of this book demonstrate, that continuous workplace renewal and reform is mandatory if organisations are to remain competitive and effective. It is clear, also, that the achievement of needed change at the 'coalface' requires active involvement of line staff in identifying aspects of workplace practice that are not functioning well and their collective search for the most feasible and desirable way of tackling these problems. This was demonstrated in Chapter 2 when discussing the tactics of start up and evaluation and in Chapter 3 when ways of enhancing the workplace milieu in education were explored.

Just as learning programs, strategic plans, workplace reforms or policy and procedure manuals developed without consulting those who are to operate them have little chance of being acted upon, so too research 'handed down from on high' from remote researchers in universities and similar places will be given scant attention by those who have not been actively involved in its design and implementation. This has been demonstrated, for example, in national evaluation studies in Switzerland and the UK which show the limited extent to which the results of research and development projects in vocational education and training have had a positive impact on practice (Scott, 1991b). It is in this context that workplace action research is now recognised as a key tool for collaborative change management in education.

Undertaking workplace action research

Workplace action research can be distinguished from the other approaches to research outlined in Table 4.1 because of the following combination of attributes:

- the ongoing identification and investigation of workplace practices requiring improvement or enhancement;
- the development of practitioners' skills in problem identification as well as in problem solving;
- unification of processes often thought to be quite disparate, for example, organisation development, curriculum change, evaluation, ethics, research and professional learning;
- surfacing and discussing which indicators should be used to judge that a change option is progressive and what, in each work context, constitutes a priority for action and what does not;
- embedding theory in practice not keeping it separate;
- ensuring that the results of inquiry actually get translated into practice (rather than, for instance, simply producing written reports on them);
- greater collaboration amongst practitioners and between practitioners and university staff;
- an emphasis on directly linking continuous professional development, learning and improved performance;
- seeking a closer alignment between organisational and individual change;
- developing strategies for change which take into account or seek to influence positively the particular culture, conditions and climate of the context(s) in which innovation is to occur.

These distinguishing characteristics of workplace action research have much in common with Donald Schön's (1983, 1987) conceptualisation of 'reflective practice' and my own research on what distinguishes effective organisational and individual change management (Scott, 1990, 1996a, 1996b). They also overlap significantly the conceptualisation of experiential learning outlined by Boud (1985). Many of these distinguishing characteristics can be traced back to the thinking of educators like John Dewey (1933) and have been specifically adapted to suit the particular focus of action research and learning in education by people like Stephen Kemmis (1985) and Kemmis and McTaggart (1988).

For further reading on the distinguishing characteristics of action research see Elliot (1991: Ch. 4) and Oja and Smulyan (1989: 10–22).

An overview of the process

How do the distinguishing characteristics of workplace action research outlined above work in practice?

Action research, like the process of continuous enhancement and innovation of which it is part, is:

- responsive to its context not inflexible;
- reciprocal not unilateral;
- cyclical and ongoing not linear and one-off;
- reflective, active and involved not rigid, passive and objective;
- team not individually based.

Figure 4.1 depicts how the process operates.[3] Note how closely this figure and the discussion which follows are related to the tactics advocated in Chapter 2 for learning program innovation and in Chapter 3 for workplace improvement in education. The figure also aligns closely with Kolb's (1984) cycle of experiential learning and anticipates the key findings of the research reviewed in the next chapter on effective change leaders, especially their skill in thinking contingently.[4] It should be emphasised, however, that the distinguishing characteristics of workplace action research are: that it occurs in the workplace; is team-based and collaborative; and is focused on continuous quality improvement of both the core activities of the service and the infrastructure which supports them.

In the ongoing, cyclical process outlined in Figure 4.1, educators are seen as being 'participant–observers' of their own practice—they *sense* when things are not going well, they work together (and with outside researchers if necessary) to identify which of these worrying aspects of practice most warrant attention. They attempt to identify the ones which, if not enhanced, are likely to have a significant and negative

Figure 4.1   The cyclical nature of workplace action research

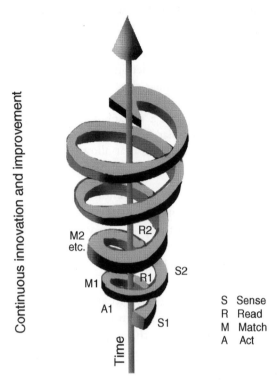

S   Sense
R   Read
M   Match
A   Act

impact on the quality of service delivery and productivity, especially the quality of their learning programs.

As they do this, they attempt to *read* (work out, detect) what lies behind the problematic situation selected. They try to figure out what is causing it, what its key dimensions are and what interpretation of the problem best fits the facts. In this way, they recognise that (in contrast to some more traditional views of research) problems in daily practice don't just present themselves on a plate—they have to be constructed from the 'swampy' and complex materials of daily practice and then given priority. That is, practitioners have to read meaning into the facts, rumours, evidence and experiences that seem to constitute a problematic area of daily practice which takes their attention. In order to make sense of what is going on they have to use 'diagnostic maps' which have been developed (learned) through reflection on previous experiences in similar (but never identical) situations. Donald Schön (1983: 138–40) describes the process as follows:

> When a practitioner makes sense of a situation he perceives to be unique, he *sees* it as something already in his repertoire . . . It is to see the unfamiliar situation as both similar to and different from the familiar one . . . The familiar situation functions as a precedent, or a metaphor, or—in Thomas Kuhn's phrase—an exemplar for the unfamiliar one . . . It is our capacity to *see-as* and *do-as* that allows us to have a feel for problems that don't fit existing rules.

Only when they have a better handle on what the problem really might be, only when they have generated an interpretation of what lies beneath the problem which tests out against the facts of their unique context, can workplace action researchers come up with what might, in practical terms, be done to improve matters. It is then that they set about designing a way of changing the situation that is causing the problem, at the same time confirming their interpretation of what the problem is. That is, they seek to 'custom tailor' or *match* a plan of action that seems to best suit the unique requirements, limits and possibilities of the situation. In this way their response is 'contingent' upon their reading of the situation.

Then they *act*—that is, they put their plan into action and assess the effects. They try to implement the solutions they think will resolve the problem and monitor the results. As they do this many unexpected but significant things may arise. In this way they ultimately come to understand the problem only by trying to change it. If their selected solutions don't work, they conclude that their interpretation of the problem was inaccurate and the spiral starts again.

In this way research, learning, action and workplace improvement are continuously intermingled in the 'spiral staircase' of continuous change depicted in Figure 4.1. Because workplace action researchers recognise that their original plan can never anticipate exactly what will happen as they try to put it into practice they are prepared to modify this plan as they try to understand and modify the aspects of daily practice they are concentrating upon. This is how the ongoing process of 'mutual adaptation', discussed in Chapter 1, is established. They come to recognise that only as they try to influence things are they able to 'illuminate' (Parlett & Dearden, 1977) what really goes on, what things really are like for the people at the 'coalface'. Figure 4.1 shows how these various phases overlap and seeks to account for the fact that the whole process of action research and learning is ongoing, cyclical and rarely linear.

Below, each aspect of the action research cycle depicted in Figure 4.1 is considered in more detail.

Sensing: identifying key dilemmas/problematic situations

Sensing a need for change is the start of the process. Practitioners sense that, from their perspective, a key aspect of daily practice just isn't 'working'. All sorts of informal as well as formal methods and indicators are used to come to this conclusion. Staff can observe, hear or read that things are not going well. If the workplace is characterised by intense and informal communication and a positive climate (see Chapter 3), this process of identifying workplace change 'hot spots' is greatly enhanced.

A central issue here is who has the right to identify the areas for enhancement in daily practice and who decides which should be given priority attention. This dilemma arises when deciding who should have the final say on what goes into a learning program (see Chapter 2) or what aspects of workplace improvement should be given priority (see Chapter 3). If the school, college, university or training unit is hierarchically structured, the identification of priorities for workplace action research should be shared between managers (who have the capacity and responsibility to ensure that action on the problems occurs) and line people (because only they know the current 'coalface' realities and because it is they who must act differently in order to resolve them).

Another key issue involves working out if the problem identified is really worth attending to. One of the key challenges in educational organisations (as noted in Chapter 3) is that they are so complex, there is so much information being generated, so much activity, so many external pressures for change, that it is hard to sort out which concerns are trivial and which are vitally important.

One way in which this phase of workplace action research can be handled systematically is to continuously monitor core activities against an agreed set of performance indicators or 'tracking measures'. This can be achieved using a monitoring approach based on the 'four level' evaluation framework discussed in Chapter 2. Such an approach would address four linked sets of education service success indicators as follows:

In order of importance:

1 The quality of the service's paperwork.
2 The extent to which the service's structure, administration, resourcing procedures, communication systems, staffing practices, incentives, climate and morale are working effectively.
3 The extent to which teachers and other staff in the service actually perform effectively and the perceived quality of its learning programs and materials.
4 The sort of impact the learning programs and associated activities have on clients and other key players.

Teams of practitioners can consider, by referring to data on these indicators, what current activities should be left as they are, which should be enhanced or which should be dropped. By looking outwards and forwards (Chapter 6) they also can identify what quite new directions are necessary. For each of the enhancements and innovations identified, they can ask questions like 'How do we know addressing this change is feasible, desirable, relevant, and distinctive?' External teams of experts can be used to check the veracity of the teams' conclusions about key change priorities and provide practical ideas on how best to act on them. It is in this way that workplace action research and external quality reviews can be more effectively linked.

If an organisation fails to develop a shared set of criteria for separating out priorities for action from 'busy work', then action research will clearly lack focus and waste time. A useful starting point is to make sure that everyone agrees on what the service's key purpose (that is, core business) is. It has already been suggested in Chapters 2 and 3 that, for educational institutions, this should be the consistent delivery of the highest quality learning programs possible, given available resources, and the continuous enhancement of the infrastructure and procedures intended to support them.

Both formal and informal means can be used to identify potential enhancement or innovation projects through workplace action research. For example, student or employer satisfaction surveys are a more formal mechanism, whereas informal chats and focus groups with students or staff are another. It is important that small, action-oriented teams of practitioners who have an interest in each enhancement or innovation are used to shape it. These teams should be temporary (that is, change specific), and 'cross functional' (that is, comprised of those people best positioned to address the particular problem area identified).

A good example of how this can be made to work in higher education was the use of Flexible Learning Action Group (FLAG) teams at the University of Technology, Sydney (UTS) in the late 1990s. Each of these teams addressed a key component of the university's move into flexible learning design and delivery. The action areas addressed included the use of interactive learning on the Internet, best practice in self-managed learning material design and the establishment of a staff web site on flexible learning. The teams were composed of people already active in the area who were charged with inventing and testing viable innovation options and then advising the university on the most feasible and desirable directions it might take in these areas.

A parallel example in school education was the Australia's Innovative Links Program which was set up by the National Schools Network. In this program university and school staff and students worked in action research teams on priority enhancement projects in the participating schools. For a detailed outline and evaluation of the approach see Scott et al. (1996). For further discussion and practical ideas on what might be done to identify and give priority to workplace problems see Elliot (1991: Ch. 6).

A prerequisite for the sort of work advocated above is that staff are willing to look critically at current practice. This was an attitude identified as an important component of a positive workplace culture in Chapter 3 and is identified as a distinguishing attribute of effective change leaders in Chapter 5. As Fullan (1993: 26) concludes:

> It seems perverse to say that problems are our friends, but we cannot . . . develop effective responses to complex situations unless we actively seek and confront the real problems which are in fact difficult to solve. Problems are our friends because it is only through immersing ourselves in problems that we can come up with creative solutions. Problems are the route to deeper change and deeper satisfaction. In this sense effective organisations 'embrace problems' rather than avoid them.

Reading: working out what the problem really is

This involves the workplace action research team diagnosing what specifically appears to be responsible for the problem identified. It entails using a range of formal and informal research strategies to gather in intelligence about what is going on in the area concerned. Tactics that could be used include referral to data generated in satisfaction surveys and focus groups, the analysis of relevant quantitative data, talking informally to key players and using the team's broader network of contacts. The general aim of this work is to 'make sense of' or 'read meaning into' the troubling situation.

As this happens, the players necessary to make the action research project a success are gradually identified. For example, in the case mentioned earlier of the UTS FLAG team using the Internet for interactive learning, an original core of three of four people gradually expanded into a series of teams totalling 40 academics undertaking a linked set of action research projects in the area.

To ensure that potentially relevant factors are not overlooked, a conceptual framework like that put forward in Chapter 1 is necessary. The change management checkpoints which summarise discussion in each section of the book give more specific guidance. For example, in the case of a learning program which is performing poorly on tracking measures like demand, student satisfaction, graduation or employment rates, the following series of checkpoints for the learning program, taken from Chapter 2, could be used to diagnose what might be responsible:

- goals and objectives;
- content;
- delivery;
- assessment methods and system;
- students;
- staff;
- learning materials;
- location;
- administration.

If the problem involves the workplace, then the following series of checkpoints for the workplace, derived from the discussion in Chapter 3, could be used to diagnose what might be responsible:

- culture and climate;
- staff selection and support procedures;
- leadership;
- mechanisms for identifying and disseminating good practice;
- communication systems;
- administrative support procedures;
- structure;
- mechanisms for monitoring the quality of what happens;

- documentation and record-keeping procedures;
- planning and decision-making approaches.

As relevant practitioners and clients are contacted to identify what, in their view, is causing the problem they can also be asked what feasibly might be done to improve matters. This starts the process of identifying potentially relevant solutions and some of the key success criteria these players will apply as the enhancement is implemented.

It may be necessary at this stage to use networks of contacts in other locations to identify what has been done elsewhere to resolve the problems identified. In this way the potential for 'groupthink', the tendency for groups to come up with solutions derived only from within the parameters of their own experience, can be avoided.

The whole process of 'reading' what is going on is reciprocal—that is, a preliminary interpretation and solution is put forward and this is tested for accuracy, appropriateness, desirability, clarity and feasibility against the facts of the workplace and the perceptions of key players. In order to engage effectively in this process of *reading and testing* an appropriate and feasible mix of data-gathering techniques must be used. These could include any of the following suggested by Elliot (1991: 77ff):

- interviews;
- focus groups;
- diaries;
- document analysis;
- photographic evidence;
- tape/video recordings and transcripts;
- using an outside observer;
- using a running commentary;
- shadowing;
- checklists, questionnaires and inventories;
- triangulation;
- analytic memos.

Gathering relevant data is not a one-off event. It is the lifeblood of all effective workplace action research. The art is to know specifically what data are needed and to use the most efficient and effective means to gather them. This was a point made when effective consultation during the start up of learning program changes was discussed in Chapter 2. If the action research team is well formed a key source of such data will be the team members themselves. However, it is important that they are not the only source.

Note that data gathering can be used not just to get in ideas but to test out the accuracy of the action research team's current reading of the problem. When its preliminary reading of the situation is complete, the team should check that this aligns with the perceptions of others. In addition this will also mean that ownership and involvement in the action research process is achieved in the ways suggested when discussing program innovations in Chapter 2. It will also demonstrate the spiralling and reciprocal character of the process.

The idea, then, is to gradually 'illuminate' what is going on and, in the light of this, gather in viable ideas on how best to address what the team believes is causing the problem. Both internal and external networks should be used to ensure that the most accurate interpretation of the problem and its possible resolution emerges. For more specific suggestions on the many data-gathering techniques ideally suited to workplace action research in education see Bell (1984: Chs 9–13)[5] and Elliot (1991: 72–5).

Having got to a point where the action research team believes it has 'read' the situation accurately and identified a potentially relevant response it is now in a position to formulate an initial plan of action.

Matching: formulating the most appropriate action plan

Here the team's focus shifts to getting ready to act. In doing this their attention is on:

- clarifying exactly what steps, actions and resources must be put in place to improve the areas for action identified during the 'sensing and reading' process;

- checking that these appear feasible;
- surfacing and making sure that what is planned matches the team's general indicators for a successfully operating education service;
- figuring out how best to support and monitor the actions and changes planned;
- continuously checking that what is planned matches the team's reading of what the change area being addressed actually encompasses.

It cannot be overemphasised that both too much and too little planning for action is counterproductive. The idea is to figure out, by picturing what will be done differently and by whom, what is likely to be the most useful and workable course of action and then to get out there and try it. The general rule, as Peters and Waterman (1984) found, is 'ready, fire, aim'. This point has already been emphasised in earlier chapters in terms of both learning and workplace changes.

It is recommended that the action plan be brief[6] (about two or three pages) and should contain:

1 A brief outline of exactly what the problem being addressed really entails, based on the team's findings during the 'sensing and reading' phase of the project.
2 A statement of precisely what is to be changed or introduced in order to improve the situation. This should be accompanied by a timeline.
3 The specific actions different team members will undertake to change things in the way envisaged.
4 An outline of the indicators that will be used to check that the proposed course of action is succeeding and a statement of how these align with agreed organisational indicators and priorities.
5 A statement of the resources that will be needed in order to undertake the proposed plan of action and who will make sure these are made available.
6 A statement of the ethical framework which will govern access to and release of any information and outcomes that

emerge.[7] As Parlett and Dearden (1977: 22), who led the way in the 1970s with research of this type in universities, emphasise: 'The price of achieving the richer, more informative data of illuminative evaluation is the greatly increased attention that must be paid to the evaluator's professional standards and behaviour.'

The following framework, adapted from the learning contract method,[8] gives some structure to the action steps in such a plan:

1 Specific objectives and tasks.
2 Required resources.
3 Who is to do this and when.
4 Indicators that will be used to judge success.

Acting: implementing the plan and evaluating the results

As the action research team's change plan is implemented, it is inevitable that not everything will go as expected. The 'swampy', complex and changing context of daily practice makes this impossible.

As Parlett and Dearden (1977: 15) found:

> The introduction of an innovation sets off a chain of repercussions throughout the learning milieu. In turn, these unintended consequences are likely to affect the innovation itself, changing its form and moderating its impact.

So, it is essential that what happens during implementation is monitored. To guide this process, the agreed indicators of a successful project developed during the 'reading' phase are used. It is essential that, as already emphasised in Chapter 2 in relation to learning program innovations, these indicators don't just look to the quality of paperwork or the fact that anticipated resources arrive when needed, but to the quality of what key players do differently and what sort of impact this is having on students, clients, productivity and the organisation's reputation. One or a mix of the techniques for gathering data outlined above may again be useful as the team seeks to monitor the implementation and impact of their improvement plan.

In the light of this evidence, modification of the action plan and the team's understanding of the problem itself may be necessary:

> There has to be a balance between front end conceptualisation and openness to promising data configurations that lead elsewhere and gradually give rise to alternative conceptualisations. (Huberman, 1987: 595)

Therefore it is highly likely, as suggested in Figure 4.1, that the action research team will have to recycle through the process a number of times in order to resolve effectively the workplace problem being addressed. Other possibilities are that, in implementing the plan, additional workplace problems of significance will emerge or the activity will trigger unintended but significant side effects or dilemmas. Either way, the team may again find itself cycling back through the action research spiral.

As the implementation of the workplace action plan proceeds, it is useful to keep a 'case record' of what was done, how effective it was, what helped or hindered the implementation of the plan, how it was modified and so on. This record can be used to disseminate an insider's picture of what is entailed in attempting to improve practice in the area identified to practitioners involved in parallel developments elsewhere.

Experiencing the process

Workplace action research involves all of the challenge, uncertainty, complexity and frustration of any change project (see Chapter 1). At the same time, it has all of the potential benefits that come from having successfully helped make a difference.

The problem with getting involved in workplace action research is poignantly described by Donald Schön (1983: 42) as follows:

In the varied topography of professional practice, there is a high, hard ground where practitioners can make effective use of research-based theory and technique, and there is a swampy lowland where situations are confusing 'messes', incapable of technical solution. The difficulty is that the problems of the high ground, however great their technical interest, are often relatively unimportant to clients or to the larger society, while in the swamp are the problems of greatest human concern. Shall the practitioner stay on the high hard ground where he can practice rigorously . . . but where he is constrained to deal with problems of relatively little social importance? Or shall he descend to the swamp where he can engage the most important and challenging problems if he is willing to forsake technical rigour?

Previous action research teams in education have described their involvement in the process as being akin to:

- swamp negotiation;
- being part of a difficult but rewarding expedition;
- engaging in a process of illumination;
- working with a group of people to build and maintain a unique structure;
- attempting to distil a fine whisky.

For everyone concerned, becoming involved in action research is never easy. Common dilemmas[9] in workplace action research have to be resolved, including how best to balance:

- prespecification of the project *with* letting the plan of action emerge as the project unfolds;
- giving senior staff who might have the power to ensure that results are acted upon the right to decide what problems are most important *with* giving decision-making power to those line staff who are closest to the realities of daily practice;
- the involvement of insiders *with* outsiders in the project;
- time on workplace action research *with* all of the other demands on our time;
- reliability (rigour) in data collection *with* validity (relevance);

- time on writing the research report *with* doing the project;
- objectivity *with* subjectivity;
- a 'warts and all' representation of what really happened *with* the need to safeguard the privacy and maintain the trust of the individuals involved.

The approach to workplace action research outlined in this chapter takes into account many of the lessons identified in earlier chapters of this book. It is a practical way of enabling educators enmeshed in a context of relentless change and faced with endless options for improvement and innovation to focus on the most important ones and, working collaboratively, to help resolve them in a way which both takes into account their own unique workplace milieu and the lessons learned by those involved in parallel initiatives elsewhere.

SHARING THE OUTCOMES OF ACTION RESEARCH PROJECTS

Both the experience of undertaking an action research project and its outcomes will be of interest to educators involved in similar change projects elsewhere. In fact, as the research on staff support reviewed in Chapter 2 reveals, it is now clear that the experience of practitioners grappling with similar problems in other locations is one of the most powerful forms of support for staff learning during implementation. As Parlett and Dearden (1977: 25) emphasise:

> Ideally, the output of . . . research will be regarded as useful, intelligible and revealing by those involved in the enterprise itself. Further, by addressing key educational issues, it can also be seen as a recognisable reality by others outside the innovation. If the report is seen merely as an arcane or irrelevant addition to a research literature already ignored by practicing educators, clearly you will have failed.

The importance of disseminating what is learned

Even though one of the most useful resources for workplace improvement or learning program changes is to access the experience of fellow educators who have already 'trod the path' in the area under investigation, there is a problem. Identifying these 'fellow travellers' is excessively difficult and finding out how they have handled common problems is often too time consuming to be feasible.

The answer is to build networks and data bases around key areas of educational innovation and enhancement more systematically. This is becoming increasingly possible and far more convenient with recent developments in using the Internet for interactive learning and to establish practitioner networks. Now it is possible for innovators from around the world who are interested in the same development area to pose questions, share strategies and work together on key change 'hot spots' from the desktop using the world wide web. One example of such a web site is the American Association for Higher Education's Technology Roundtable which operates across the world out of Washington DC. Another example is the joint Ontario Teachers Federation and Ontario Institute for Studies in Education (OISE) electronic learning network for teachers which commenced operation in Canada in the early 1990s.

To assist in this work, the achievements of successful workplace action research projects in education need to be documented in a way which is useful for fellow practitioners. These case histories can then be used to build up searchable data bases accessible from Internet sites like those above. A framework for a 'user friendly' form of documentation is suggested below.

The case study approach

An ideal vehicle for documenting and disseminating what is learned from workplace action research and improvement projects in education is to use a case study approach. The case study has the advantage of capturing the 'real life' quality of what happened as the process unfolded and, as a consequence, can present the lessons learned in an authentic and relevant way.

When compiling a workplace action research case study, the useful components of such a framework[10] should include:

- The nature of the workplace problem addressed and why it was so important to act in relation to it.
- What tactics and methods were used to clarify and test the team's interpretation of the problem and to gather ideas on how to overcome it.
- Which of these tactics and methods worked well and which did not.
- What plan of action was eventually adopted to address the problem and which aspects of this worked well and which did not.
- The indicators of 'success' that the team used to monitor what happened as the plan of action was implemented. What had to be changed as a result of this monitoring and what worked effectively.
- What sorts of implementation support tactics the action-research team would recommend to others interested in similar projects.
- How the team's understanding of the problem evolved over time.
- What unexpected but significant things happened as a result of the project and an explanation of why these were significant.
- Any ethical dilemmas which arose and how they were resolved.
- Difficulties which arose in trying to work collaboratively as an action research team and how/if these were resolved.
- A brief discussion of how effective the action-research framework contained in this chapter proved to be and how, in the light of the team's experience in using it, it might need to be modified.

Stenhouse (1978) makes a useful distinction between *case data*, a *case record* and a *case study*. In workplace action research, *case data* is all the evidence collected in the reading, matching and acting phases illustrated in Figure 4.1. It can be in the form of recordings, transcripts, diaries, notes, photographs, video tapes and so on. These data are clustered in terms of their relevance to the key issues addressed, those which arose in the project and according to the components listed above. The *case record* is a running compilation of the case data. The *case study* is the analysis of this case record. It is the attempt to make sense of the team's experience to date and to draw out the key lessons learned.

Miles and Huberman (1984) give extensive practical ideas on how best to move from 'raw' case data to a final case study. Winter (1989: Ch. 8) provides a case study of how he actually wrote up one of his action research projects.

Using video and photographs

If the resources are available, a video which shows the action research project in operation and includes interviews with key players commenting on what happened has also been found to be a useful medium for dissemination. The video *Breaking New Ground* (Scott, Wickert & Courtenay, 1992), for example, reports on an action research project involving a vocational education institute's initiatives in the establishment of fee-for-service courses. *Competence in Practice* (Scott & Wickert, 1993) traces the development of new approaches to curriculum design and assessment in an automotive department at a TAFE college.

Another medium for disseminating the outcomes of workplace action research is the photograph. An example of a workplace research project which used this medium is *Focal Points* (Scott & McDonald, 1988). This workplace research project investigated and documented a wide range of alternative teaching and learning strategies in TAFE and Adult Education.

Research on the effective dissemination of research and development projects in education

Simply producing a well written and accessible case study or a well made film is not enough to ensure effective dissemination of the outcomes of an action research project. In fact one of the recurring problems with federally funded innovations programs in education is that the outcomes of specific projects rarely go beyond the people who have received the funding. Additional tactics and factors are necessary.

In a review of research on successful dissemination strategies for research and development projects in vocational education and training (Scott, 1991b) the following factors and tactics were found to be significant:

- Using communication strategies that go well beyond the written word, in particular dissemination by 'word of mouth' through highly active informal and formal contact networks.
- The existence of close ongoing links between university researchers and practitioners in the field.
- Ensuring that organisational rewards, incentives and structure support action research, and continuous enhancement in the area(s) of practice being addressed.
- Adoption of a variety of non-traditional staff development strategies, including staff exchanges and the establishment of 'buddy' systems between centres.
- The presence of key people with dissemination and utilisation 'savviness' in each workplace.
- The establishment of specific dissemination and implementation agencies by umbrella organisations and professional associations.
- Convenient access to proven change ideas via, for instance, electronic learning networks.

Many of these dissemination factors could, themselves, become the subject of more detailed action research. More generally, there is a need for those bodies who fund research and development projects in education to apply these findings as they commission and assess projects.

Mini workplace action research project

This is intended to be a very small, pilot project only, one in which you briefly try out the workplace action research cycle outlined in this chapter and evaluate what happened. To do this:

1 Re-read the relevant sections of this chapter to make sure you are clear on what workplace action research is all about. In particular study Figure 4.1 which describes the workplace action research cycle and the discussion that follows.
2 Using checkpoints for improvement included in this chapter as a guide, identify one aspect of your workplace's operation which you sense needs investigation and enhancement.
3 With one or two colleagues who share this interest, move through at least one cycle of the phases of sensing, reading, matching and acting, documenting what happens as you go.
4 Reflect on what happened as you attempted to move through the process, identifying one or two things that impressed you and one or two that did not, using the list of common dilemmas in workplace action research as a guide.

LOCATING AND REVIEWING RESEARCH ARTICLES ON EDUCATIONAL CHANGE

During the 'matching' phase of workplace action research it is often important to look at what others have discovered about the effective management of the change being addressed. It is important, therefore, that the staff involved possess the necessary skills to efficiently and effectively locate and review relevant educational research. In doing this it is especially important that they are able to distinguish between well founded and trivial change research.

Locating potentially relevant research studies on educational change

Large amounts of time can be wasted trying to locate high quality research relevant to a specific educational or workplace improvement. It is often through well developed networks of practitioners that educators are best able to locate such material. However, there are occasions when such networks do not deliver and one needs to use a literature search. There are a number of computer searchable data bases in education which can make this job much easier than the old manual searches. For example there is the ERIC[11] data base and the Australian Education Index. The options are expanding quickly as more and more searchable CD data bases are coming on line.

In general terms, these data bases allocate 'descriptors' (key words) which identify the main focus of each piece of work reviewed. They include an abstract of the work and its bibliographic details. Data bases like ERIC are searchable by computer. In order to make a search efficient it is necessary to pick out the combination of descriptors which, together, identify exactly what you are looking for. For example, below is an example of a search of ERIC looking for research articles on the change process in post-secondary education. Notice how a number of relevant 'descriptors' (lines 1–10) have been selected from the ERIC Thesaurus of Descriptors. Then the intersection between particular combinations of these and the descriptor 'research' (line 12) has been entered. When the search of ERIC commences, only articles with the specified combination codes attached to them will be identified.

```
No.      Records  Request
1:       602      CHANGE-AGENTS
2:       146      COMMUNITY-CHANGE
3:       2664     CHANGE-STRATEGIES
4:       3223     CHANGE-AGENTS or COMMUNITY-CHANGE or
                  CHANGE-STRATEGIES
5:       1293     TECHNICAL-EDUCATION
6:       6423     VOCATIONAL-EDUCATION
7:       15566    COLLEGES
8:       7627     UNIVERSITIES
9:       57093    HIGHER-EDUCATION
10:      70870    TECHNICAL-EDUCATION or VOCATIONAL-
                  EDUCATION or COLLEGES or UNIVERSITIES or
                  HIGHER-EDUCATION
11:      1195     #10 and #4
12:      108538   RESEARCH
13:      488      #11 and RESEARCH
14:      96008    FI=ED
15:      382      #13 and FI=ED
16:      106      #13 not #15
```

Notice how one has the choice of searching for alternative descriptors (line 1 or 2 or 3; line 5 or 6 or 7 or 8 or 9), of then combining these (line 11) and checking that every article identified is also about research (line 12). The greater the number of descriptors used the more likely one is to identify only those articles of immediate relevance.

The results of the search (in the form of an abstract for each document and its bibliographic details) can be provided to the desktop electronically, usually in a form compatible with your word processing program. This means the results can be checked and manipulated in the same way as any other word processing file. The articles identified can be culled by referring to the abstracts provided and notes can be added as necessary.

Below is a 'print-out' of the information given for each ERIC hit. The notes in bold type and italics were added as the information was reviewed, as shown on the next page.

The bibliographic information for the final selection of articles can then be used to locate the articles themselves. In

AN: EJ397967

Relevance: Appears to be particularly relevant—covers importance of vision and principles as well as the techniques for managing desired changes in the Canadian equivalent of TAFE Colleges.

AU: Levin,-John-S; Dennison,-John-D.
TI: **Responsiveness and Renewal in Canada's Community Colleges: A Study of Change in Organisations.**
PY: 1989
JN: Canadian-Journal-of-Higher-Education; v19 n2 p41-57 1989
AV: UMI
AB: A study examined the extent to which Canada's community colleges have retained their 1960s founding principles in adapting to economic and socio-political change of the 1980s. *It found much of the original idealism and innovation, but also several diverse ways of adjusting and a variety of techniques for managing those changes.*

some institutions an on-line ordering service makes this process very convenient. Articles may be available in electronic form over the Internet (from the so-called electronic journals[12]), in full text from a CD Rom,[13] on microfiche or in traditional print form.

Reviewing research systematically

Two aspects of any research article can be reviewed: its methodological and conceptual quality as a piece of research, and the usefulness and relevance of its results. There is a tendency for many educators to ignore the first aspect when they review research. Yet it is unwise to accept as valid or reliable a set of results which may have been generated using questionable means even if, on face value, they seem attractive.

Reviewing the conceptual and methodological quality of a research article

Here the nature and quality of a research study is examined. This includes an assessment of:

■ Its setting (for example, its country of origin, the sector of education studied, how compatible the study's setting is with the one under investigation).

- Its research design (for example, does it use a longitudinal case study, a retrospective case study, a survey, an experiment, a piece of action research, an ethnography, another technique or a combination of approaches? How appropriate is the chosen design to the stated purposes of the study?).

- Its conception (for example, is a conceptual framework used to guide the study and to make sense of the data generated? Are research assumptions surfaced?).

- Data sources (for example, what sorts of people, documents or other sources are consulted?).

- Sampling procedure (for example, how representative is the sample, and how important is representativeness in this case?).

- Methods used to collect data (for example, document analysis, self-report, interview, questionnaire, direct observation, sociogram etc. How reliable and appropriate are these methods?).

- Methods used to analyse data (for example, procedures used to distil, make sense of data and present results. How reliable and appropriate are these methods?).

Some studies may say little about the above matters, others give a much fuller explanation. The overall objective should be to identify studies that seem to be well conceived, give a clear indication of how they were carried out and provide evidence that this was both appropriate and reliably implemented.

If a number of studies are being reviewed, their position in relation to each of the above methodological checkpoints can be presented in tabular form. This allows the reader to get a quick overall feel for the comparative methodological and conceptual quality of the studies reviewed. A decision can then be made about which results are most soundly based. The key point to keep in mind in this phase of the review process is that just because something is in print doesn't automatically mean that its conclusions were soundly determined.

Reviewing the results of the research article

If, after the above tests are applied, a particular article does appear to be conceptually and methodologically sound, then one can proceed to review (that is, interpret and make judgments about) its findings. Usually the reviewer will be looking for specific insights about particular questions. These should be clear from the outset (as indicated when discussing the importance of specifying descriptors in an ERIC search). That is, when the results of a piece of change research are reviewed it should always be with a specific purpose in mind. Random, purposeless professional reading, is inefficient.

For example, questions like the following could be asked:

- How do these results give insights into the specific improvement or innovation problem I am addressing?
- Where do these results fit into the change management framework outlined in Chapter 1? Do they provide additional insights not accounted for in that framework? In which case how can the framework be modified to accommodate them?

CONCLUSION

To effectively manage the process of continuous quality improvement and innovation in both learning programs and organisational support, a change tool which is collaborative, efficient and action-oriented is necessary. It has been proposed in this chapter that workplace action research, an approach which has a long and proven history, matches these requirements.

If the spiralling approach of workplace action research is to be effective, however, explicit attention must be given to how it is deployed.

First, workplace action-research groups need to be used judiciously and strategically. Organisational leaders, in consultation with staff and students, need to determine what constitutes an achievable and focused set of strategic development priorities and then restrict the commissioning of workplace action-research groups to these. People do not have the time to participate in endless workplace action-research groups, especially ones which have no clear strategic benefit or are unsupported by key organisational figures.

Second, particular attention must be given to figuring out who should make up each action-research team. Action research by committee will not work. Participants must be those people who have a stake in making the change project work and who are best positioned to act on its outcomes. For example, they need to be actively involved in and committed to change in the area concerned and to occupy one of the teaching or administrative roles essential to its success. It is in this way that appropriately constituted action-research teams are 'cross-functional'.

Third, simply forming an action-research group is not enough. Those involved will need explicit coaching on how best to use the approach. Here case studies from previous action-research groups, shaped along the lines suggested in this chapter, can be a valuable resource. In particular, team members will need to be alerted to both the benefits and pitfalls of collaborative work and group dynamics.

Finally, as we saw when discussing the application of this technique to program start up and implementation, each action-research team requires the active support of a senior organisational mentor. This is someone who publicly promotes and acknowledges what they do and who ensures that the results of their work are effectively supported and disseminated.

Of particular importance is the way in which such 'cross-functional' teams might best learn from those involved in similar change projects. The chapter has, for example, addressed the important need to train staff on how best to locate, retrieve and assess the quality of change research using recent, rapid developments in information technology. If case studies of successful action-research projects are documented along the lines suggested in this chapter, and if these are made available using the new capabilities for interactive learning on the Internet, then the process of dissemination and utilisation of such work will be greatly enhanced.

The guidelines for efficient information access and assessment outlined in this chapter identify what might best be covered in sorely needed staff learning programs concerning information technology literacy and change in education.

When well managed, workplace action research, with its focus on achieving practical change on key strategic improvements, is one of the most effective staff development tools available. Fullan (1991: Ch. 15) provides numerous case studies and cites research which confirms this proposition. In the following chapter the links between action research, change management and effective individual professional learning are explored in more detail. In Chapter 6 another relevant key tool—the use of strategic networking—is introduced.

So far we've explored what makes for effective learning program change (Chapter 2), successful workplace improvement (Chapter 3) and effective action research (Chapter 4). However, as Chapter 1 emphasised, educational changes do not unfold spontaneously, they have to be led. The knowledge and skills discussed in Chapters 2 and 4 have to be identified and developed in staff and applied wisely. For this to occur, effective change leaders must be present. It is to the research and practice of effective change leadership and professional learning in education that we now turn.

5

THE EFFECTIVE
LEADER OF CHANGE

*At its heart, the traditional view of leadership
is based on assumptions of people's powerlessness,
their lack of personal vision and inability to master
forces of change, deficits which can be remedied only by
a few great leaders . . . The new view of leadership in
learning organisations centres on subtler and more important
tasks. In a learning organisation leaders are designers,
stewards and teachers.*

P. Senge (1990)

The idea that only the 'boss' should look after necessary
change and that everyone else should await and obey orders
no longer fits what is needed for organisations to survive and
thrive in the late twentieth century. 'Learning organisations'
(Senge, 1990) feature people who, at all levels, embrace and
work effectively with change. In this sense, everyone has to
see themselves as a leader of continuous change, learning and
improvement in their own area of responsibility and expertise.

There should also be little doubt by now that involvement
in continuous change is inevitable:

Managers and their organizations are confronting wave upon
wave of change in the form of new technologies, markets,
forms of competition, social relations, forms of organization

147

and management, ideas and beliefs and so on. Wherever one looks, one sees a new wave coming. And it is vitally important that they accept this as a fundamental aspect of their reality, rise to the challenge, and learn to ride or moderate these waves with accomplishment. (Morgan, 1988: xii)

We now know that possessing the knowledge and skills outlined in the first four chapters of this book is necessary for educators to contribute to the effective management of ongoing change at their education service and in their own area of professional expertise. But it is not sufficient. They need something in addition if they are to apply and update this knowledge appropriately. These extra, personal attributes concern:

- their stance towards change, work and the people who populate it;
- their ability to think creatively, reflectively and with focus, especially their ability to 'read and match';
- their ability to continuously update what they know and can do, especially through their expertise in the self-management of their career-long learning.

Without these attributes they will not be able, in Morgan's analogy, to ride the many waves of change that will inevitably and consistently come upon them in the coming years. It is insufficient to become skilled only at being a commentator on the waves of change, sitting on the shore explaining where they come from and what effect they are having on others. Educators must also be capable of getting in there themselves and riding the waves of change with accomplishment.

The perspective on effective change leadership in education put forward in this chapter is succinctly outlined by Binney and Williams (1995: 52):

'Leaning into the future' recognises that effective leadership of change involves bringing together apparently contradictory qualities. Successful leaders shape the future *and* they adapt to the world as it is. They are clear about what they want to change *and* they are responsive to others' views and concerns. They are passionate about the direction in which they want the organisation to go *and* they understand and value the

148

current reality of the organisation, why it has been successful and what its people are good at. They lead *and* learn.

The image of a person leaning forward captures our view. To lean as far forward as you can requires you to have both feet firmly on the ground—stand on tip toe and you topple over.

What is intriguing is the power of the combination, of the *ands*.

In what follows, the capabilities necessary for educators to lead organisational change and manage their own career-long learning will be introduced. Readers will be invited to surface their view of what attributes distinguish an effective change leader in education and then to compare their view with what research has found. Finally, the tactics and support needed to develop competence as a career-long learner also will be discussed.

It is important to keep in mind that, when considering what is presented in the chapter, as many people as possible in as many roles as possible in an education service should possess the leadership and self-managed learning attributes discussed, not just the senior staff. That is, as many people as possible need to possess the common stance and way of thinking outlined in this chapter and be able to apply these attributes to handling continuous change with aplomb both organisationally and personally.

PROFILE OF THE EFFECTIVE LEADER IN AN EDUCATION SERVICE

What, for you, distinguishes the most effective educational leaders you have encountered from the least effective ones?

The effective educational leader

Think back over your career in education or training. Try to identify the most effective leader you have encountered and the least effective one.

1 What was it about the most effective leader that distinguished him/her from the least effective one?

2 Compare and contrast your results with the leadership research outlined below.

3 In the light of this identify the key leadership attributes you believe you should exemplify when next involved in educational change, noting your current areas of strength and areas for further development.

There is a repeated pattern in research and writing on the most capable educational leaders and practitioners.[1] In general, the relentless inevitability of change means that effective leaders must also be effective managers of change. The same goes for the most successful teachers and people in other educational roles.

The results of research on the distinctive attributes, skills and knowledge of effective change leaders is summarised below. Note how closely the profile aligns with that of the effective teacher.

The *stance* of the effective leader of educational change:

- gives positive support and doesn't put people down;
- treats staff as equals—listens generously;
- is organised and efficient (but not overly so);
- is enthusiastic and cares about education;
- has a sense of humour/perspective;
- is committed to doing things well;
- perseveres and doesn't overreact when things go wrong;
- can tolerate ambiguity, doesn't try to force own point of view or always win the argument;
- is willing to experiment and take sensible risks;
- has wider interests than just work—can put work into a broader perspective;
- is willing to learn from errors;
- accepts change as inevitable;
- is action-oriented and committed to lead by example.

The effective leader's *way of thinking*:

- sees each situation as both a unique case and as potentially similar to previous ones;
- prepares for and manages change by accurately 'reading

and matching'. Uses a well developed repertoire of 'diagnostic maps' to do this;

- is imaginative, flexible and allows for thinking on your feet as a change is implemented; can effectively reflect in action;
- is capable of thinking things through, of tracing out the consequences of different possibilities;
- can get to the nub of a problem situation and anticipate upcoming difficulties;
- can learn effectively from experience (reflects on experience using a framework);
- can effectively direct and monitor his/her own ongoing professional learning.

The required *knowledge and skills* of the effective leader of educational change:

- understands and can work with the dynamics of the change process (see Chapter 1);
- knows all the key influences which may have to be taken into account in each change situation;
- understands the nature and processes of learning program design, implementation and evaluation (see Chapter 2) and of organisational enhancement (see Chapter 3);
- understands the dynamics and tactics of workplace action research (see Chapter 4);
- knows how best to document and disseminate the outcomes of each change effort (see Chapter 4);
- is able to look outwards and to the future as well as inwards and to the present (see Chapter 6);
- possesses the wide variety of skills needed for effectively involving, negotiating with and delegating to key players in the change process (one-on-one, in small groups and in meetings);[2]
- possesses a wide repertoire of communication skills suited to both formal and informal contexts[3] (these would include the skills needed to cope with micropolitics[4] and to 'network');
- can set up and sustain a constructive working climate;[5]

151

- has a firm grasp of current knowledge and practice in his/her area of teaching;
- understands how the process of teaching and learning works. Possesses a wide repertoire of the tactics known to promote effective learning;
- can effectively use appropriate technology to enhance efficiency in all aspects of work and in personal professional learning;
- understands the nature and tactics of effective self-managed professional learning.

What is summarised above gives a broad picture of the capabilities necessary to successfully negotiate, lead and manage in the constantly changing daily realities of work in education at the end of the twentieth century. It is clear from studying this that performance skills and knowledge are important components. However it is also clear that one must also possess 'higher order' attributes like stance and way of thinking. Possession of performance skills and professional knowledge without the ability to work out when and when not to use them may indicate technical proficiency but does not guarantee an ability to lead change effectively. As Michael Fullan (1997: 6) observes:

> We all know smart people who do dumb things (Feinberg & Tarrant, 1995) and that many people of modest intelligence are quite successful . . . The combination of heart and head is crucial to effectiveness . . . Hope is not a naive, sunny view of life. It is the capacity not to panic in tight situations, to find ways and resources to address difficult problems.

The idea that professional competence (capability) requires all of the components outlined (stance, way of thinking, performance skills and professional knowledge) finds considerable support in recent research and writing.[6]

The necessary performance skills and knowledge identified above have already been discussed in great detail in earlier chapters. Stance and way of thinking, however, warrant more detailed discussion here because they have been less well explored in spite of their crucial role in effective change management.

Stance

When people are set the task of identifying what distinguishes really effective leaders of change and successful practitioners in education from their less capable counterparts, they almost always start by talking about their stance. That is, they usually start by discussing the *affective* or emotional side of the top performers they have encountered. They discuss how these individuals position themselves in relation to life at work and to the people who populate it. As Binney and Williams (1995: 59–61) found:

> The behaviour of leaders under pressure provides insights into their underlying beliefs and commitment. It also highlights the underlying patterns of individual behaviour, as we tend to 'revert to type' when we feel under pressure . . . One essential ingredient is . . . to take risks, to experiment, to encourage others to experiment and to support them if things get difficult . . . Consistent, visible behaviour sends powerful signals around the organisation and has a greater effect than 'glossy' visions.

People who find it difficult to tolerate ambiguity and uncertainty, who panic when things go wrong, who always want to win a point or have their own way, people who are unwilling to acknowledge and learn from their errors, who find it difficult to treat staff and clients in a sensitive and supportive fashion will consistently be rated by colleagues as ineffective when change is in the air. Nor does such a stance enable them to grow professionally as individuals.

This is as true for other life roles as it is for work:

> There is a natural connection between a person's work life and all other aspects of life. We live only one life, but for a long time our organisations have operated as if this simple fact could be ignored, as if we had two separate lives. (Senge, 1990: 307)

Being willing to listen genuinely and with empathy, especially to 'resistors', is a key attribute of the stance necessary to manage change effectively. In this case:

> The challenge is to turn this negative energy to a constructive purpose. Often this is not difficult. What is needed is to hear the discontent, not to judge or deny it, but accept that it is what others perceive. This simple act of listening, of seeking to understand the nature of the discontent, is enough to begin to shift staff's perception. (Binney & Williams, 1995: 104)

Stance may be hard to measure but it is arguably at the core of the individual's ability to lead and manage ongoing personal and educational change and improvement. Consider, for example, the following comments made by experienced deans during a leadership study in an Australian university (Scott & Kemmis, 1996: 8):[7]

Tolerance for uncertainty and ambiguity

> You have to be able to handle ambiguity. There are so many situations where there is not a clear answer or a policy. So you have to make judgments and must live with the consequences.
>
> You must be willing to accept the unexpected.
>
> When things go wrong, as they inevitably will, you have to be calm in the way you relate to others and remain calm within. Panic does not make for wise outcomes.
>
> I don't make decisions on the spot. I always try to get all sides of the story first and think about it overnight if possible. This willingness to suspend judgment is important.

Sensitivity to others

> A large proportion of the job is about relationships.
>
> People will come to you with teaching, scholarship or personal problems. You have to be willing to find out about their problem and then must decide whether or not to intervene.
>
> It is important to have broad humanistic qualities: to care about people, have empathy with their situation.

Listening is a key attribute. Always listen first but then be willing to take the hard decision.

People don't respond well to others who pass the buck up or the blame down.

You'll encounter all types. The key challenge is being able to work productively with all this diversity.

It is essential to be even-handed and not to make decisions based on dislike of individuals or programs.

The best attitude is not 'what's in it for me' but 'how will we all benefit?'

Approachability, discretion, consistency, openness and trustworthiness is what people look for. They don't like devious people.

Commitment to collaborative relationships

Trust is vital—staff have to trust you and you have to trust staff.

You must have the capacity to keep a confidence.

People don't like it all being done by the dean. You must be able to trust people and delegate. Let people have their jobs.

Deans that keep everything to themselves because they believe others can't be trusted burn out.

Lead by example not by mandate.

Risk taking and perseverance

You have to be willing to take sensible risks.

You need stamina. You have to be in it for the long term.

In some cases you have to be prepared to ask for forgiveness rather than permission.

A secure sense of self

You need a strong inner core to handle the day-to-day pressures and uncertainties of the job.

You can't be too thin-skinned or take everything personally. A lot of the time people are reacting to the role not to you as an individual.

If you want to always be popular you'll have problems.

A sense of humility is important.

Be willing to admit weaknesses and that you are wrong. This, ironically, is a sign of strength.

You have to be willing to take responsibility.

155

Avoid defensiveness or coming across as always having to be right.

Perspective

You need a sense of humour and a capacity to grin.

My approach to work is not to strive for 100 per cent quality if 50 per cent of the effort will give me 90 per cent quality.

Individuals who work 24 hours a day reveal a difficulty in either working out what's important or in letting go.

Balance is essential. I have a really strong sense of self-preservation. If I do start to feel overwhelmed I take some time out.

I switch off after I leave work. I'm a bit phlegmatic at home.

Way of thinking

Michael Fullan (1997) addresses the cognitive capabilities of the effective and creative change leader. He quotes Csikszentmihalyi (1996: 365):

> [Creative people] do not rush to define the nature of problems; they look at the situation from various angles first and leave the formulation undetermined for a long time. They consider different causes and reasons. They test their hunches about what is really going on, first in their own mind, and then in reality. They try tentative solutions and check their success—and they are open to reformulating the problem if the evidence suggests they started out onto the wrong path.

How educators think through what is likely to be the most appropriate course of action when involved in change is of equal importance. Those who are rated as being best at managing ongoing organisational, educational and personal change are described variously as having a 'creative intelligence', as being able to 'think on their feet', as being people who 'anticipate problems' and who can consistently come up with an accurate interpretation of what is the most sensible thing to do in each situation. Some people describe them as being 'reflective thinkers', 'good at detection' or as having an 'adaptable way of thinking'. When asked to describe how they move from sensing a problem to handling it effectively, they talk about a contingent process of thinking very similar to that which underpins the tactics of workplace action research outlined in Chapter 4 and the process of 'reading and matching' introduced in Chapter 2.[8]

The leaders who rate worst are seen to be 'rigid' in their thinking, to have a 'regurgitative' (as distinct from a 'creative') intelligence, to react always in the same way irrespective of the situation, to misread motives, to be unable to see the consequences of their actions and so on. Given the 'swampy' reality of daily life in education and the diversity of indicators of effectiveness different players use (see Chapters 1 and 2) as well as the constantly changing milieu in which it must operate (see Chapter 3), people who are 'set in their ways', who don't see or who ignore the approaching 'waves of change' or who respond unimaginatively or unreflectively cannot expect to cope.

Consider, for example, the observations made by the deans in the study of university leadership (Scott & Kemmis, 1996: 9):

Contingent thinking

You have to be pragmatic. I'm a bit sceptical about the idea of a master plan. You do need a vision but this can't be set in concrete—things change too rapidly for that.

There's no one correct way—it all depends on the particular situation.

What I would do if I were a new dean would be driven by my diagnosis of where the faculty is at. I'd look at things like the strategic plan, key outside and inside issues, and the new directions in which the faculty is being pushed or pulled.

You have to be able to pick your right game.

'Seeing the forest for the trees'

Vision is the top of my list, that is, you have to have somewhere for the faculty to be heading and through collegial processes work out why this is relevant and then take them there.

Understand that a lot of activities are tied—research, teaching, enrolments, structure, morale, resources, administration etc.

If you can't see the big picture you'll never manage your time effectively.

The skill is to avoid becoming buried in minutiae.

You have to simultaneously keep an eye on the faculty, the university and what's going on outside.

You have to work out 'who are my customers and stakeholders?' Give this deep thought.

Determining priorities for action

The job is really about how to pick the winners.

It requires the capacity to assign probabilities. For example, to figure out when to go with something and when to hold back.

You need to be 'plugged into' the right networks.

You have to be able to recognise when your efforts will be a waste of time.

If you took everything in your in-tray seriously there's a 40-hour job just there . . . So you need to be good at making judgments about significance.

It is essential that decisions are taken—it is no good to simply be a good listener or to take advice or to have consultative meetings. Ultimately you are responsible for action.

Identifying talent and making links

The aim is to identify the right people for the right roles.

Deans are the key link between the academic area and overall administration. You must understand the two worlds and connect them.

Tracing out the consequences

People will come in and be passionate. Before I decide if I should go with them I check it out, think it through.

What looks like a good idea on the surface sometimes has hidden traps which aren't at first apparent.

What does this 'creative', 'reflective', 'contingent' way of thinking entail? Studies over the past decade have started to give us a clearer understanding of what is going on in the successful change leader's mind. It seems that such people are continuously engaging in a process of 'reading and matching' (Hunt, 1987: Ch. 4). This process was first noted when effective approaches to program design were identified in Chapter 2 and was discussed further when the cyclic approach to workplace action research was outlined in Chapter 4.

As we saw in Chapter 2, when the most effective educational programmers first sense a need for a learning program change (for example, a need to create a new learning program or to modify an existing one), they start the design process by scanning the external, system and local contexts (using diagnostic maps developed from previous experience and frameworks such as that put forward in Chapter 1 of this book). They do this to figure out what must be taken into account and what is most likely to work effectively. They scan all aspects of their current context—all the people who have a stake in the learning program, their operating context and broader factors that might have to be taken into account. What they are trying to do, as we saw in Chapter 4, is to 'make sense' of a highly complex number of factors by 'reading meaning' into the unique situation, much in the same way as one reads meaning into or makes sense of a book.

Effective change leaders do this in order to work out what way of proceeding will best 'match' the unique requirements of their setting. They are also trying to work out if conditions are ripe for the innovation to proceed (that is, that it is feasible, desirable, relevant and distinctive). This process of 'reading and matching' is complex and, typically, intuitive. The present (and unique) situation is seen as being similar to (but never exactly the same as) a previous one. Once they see it as somewhat like a previous case, practitioners with this way of thinking have an idea of what to do, because they recall what worked, or what they decided had to be done differently after reflecting on the previous case. Of course, what they decide to do in the present situation will never be exactly the same as before because each educational circumstance is always a bit different from another. Schön (1983, 1987) calls this process 'see as—do as'. This way of thinking about change situations is identical to that used by teams which are skilled in program innovation (see Chapter 2) and in workplace action research (see Chapter 4).

For example, in the start-up phase of program design effective change leaders are involved in a process of 'reflection *before* action'. And the same process of sensing, reading and matching applies in the way they handle the challenge of identifying and developing structural, cultural or administrative reforms in their service. Their focus is particularly on working out what the problem really is, on what *lies behind* the dilemma or situation that triggered a need for change. What they are engaged in, therefore, is not so much a process of 'problem solving' as 'problem construction', something often ignored in discussions of professional competence.

Why is the process of problem construction (that is, 'reading and matching') so important? As was pointed out in Chapters 1 to 3, life in education is so variable, complex and ambiguous that teaching, learning or organisational problems simply can't be expected to present themselves in an unambiguous way. The problem most of the time is that, when dilemmas present themselves, educators can't work out what the problem is—all they know is that things are not going as expected, that something is amiss. The real challenge, as Chapter 4 indicates, is to work out what the problem really is, that is, to try to read meaning into the situation with some accuracy. Only after they have done the work of problem construction, only after they have 'read' what is happening and have 'matched' (decided upon) a suitable response, must educators then have a well developed repertoire of performance skills to call upon. That is, they not only need to work out what to do but they then have to be able to skilfully 'deliver the goods'.

A similar process occurs once these effective educational change managers start to work with others to put their plan into action, whether it be a program innovation or a workplace improvement. Their stance enables them to accept that not everything will go according to plan, that there will always be some sort of unique twist or unexpected dilemma once the innovation is underway. They know that many dilemmas have to be resolved 'on the spot', and that they will have to 'reflect-in-action' to do this. As we saw in relation to learning program implementation in Chapter 2, to do this they often scan previous patterns of experience (diagnostic maps) to determine if the situation being faced is one they've encountered before. If they recall something with a similar pattern, they have a way of working out what might lie behind the problem and, in consequence, to identify a way out of it.

The whole process of 'reading, matching and acting' is cyclical and holistic, not linear. The practitioner experiences a dilemma, tries to make sense of what the problem really is by using a repertoire of diagnostic maps. This gives insights into what might be done, the practitioner tries this and evaluates the results. If the dilemma remains, the practitioner recycles through the process again. This is precisely what characterises the approach to workplace action research (see Chapter 4). This is why effective change management and effective workplace action research are so closely intertwined. As Schön (1983: 132) emphasises:

> The process spirals through stages of appreciation, action and re-appreciation. The unique and uncertain situation comes to be understood through the attempt to change it and changed through the attempt to understand it.

The cycle of thinking by *reflecting-in-action* can be depicted as shown in Figure 5.1. Clearly if it is possible to bring together change teams whose members all possess the sorts of attributes being discussed, then the chances of creative and effective solutions to change problems will be optimised. It is in this way that individual and organisational change are inextricably linked.

Figure 5.1   Reflection-in-action

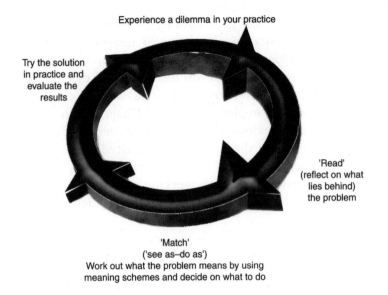

Experience a dilemma in your practice

Try the solution in practice and evaluate the results

'Read' (reflect on what lies behind) the problem

'Match' ('see as–do as') Work out what the problem means by using meaning schemes and decide on what to do

Learning from experience

How do effective managers of ongoing educational change develop the 'diagnostic maps' (meaning-giving schemes) with which they make sense of what lies behind change situations? First, they need to have had previous experience working in situations similar to their present one. Second, they need to have reflected on this previous experience, to have worked out why things went well or why they didn't. This learning from experience is best done if they use overall frameworks like those put forward in this book.

This idea of learning through reflection on experience is discussed in some detail by Boud (1985). The more a current situation varies from the ones previously experienced the more people feel 'at sea'. This is what happens when people first start teaching or become an educational manager. They are uncertain because they are yet to build up the relevant 'diagnostic maps' with which to make sense of what is happening, they are yet to learn to recognise what the signs mean and to figure out what might be the best way to act.

If educators never try new approaches, never reflect on experience, never compare their experience with overviews of 'best practice', never talk with colleagues about what does or doesn't work, and if they never see colleagues in action, then the chances that they will build up a well developed repertoire of 'diagnostic maps' is significantly decreased. This is why effective educators aren't just people with lots of experience, they are people who have reflected on that experience, people who have taken sensible risks, who have learned from their errors, who have considered the consequences. They are people who are constantly trying to improve and expand their understanding of practice. This is why stance is so central to developing professional competence.

'Diagnostic maps', like stance, are closely tied up with assumptions about what constitutes 'effective' education. This is because, given that educators use their different diagnostic maps to make sense of what is going on in a situation, they are simultaneously making judgments about what is worth attending to and what is not. In this way 'reading and matching' is closely aligned with the ongoing process of informal evaluation noted in Chapter 2. This is why, in order to be clear on what they are trying to achieve, they need to surface and critique their assumptions about what constitutes 'good and bad' education and their assumptions about what constitutes a competent teacher, student or staff member. In general, the ability to learn from experience in the ways outlined above is one of the most powerful forms of self-managed professional learning available.

In summary, the most effective leaders and managers of ongoing change, like the people occupying *all* the roles in an education service, need to possess a wide range of performance skills specifically relevant to their particular role and context. They must also have sound and relevant professional knowledge and possess key generic skills (like the ability to use computers) and knowledge (like an understanding of human motivation and effective change management).

Figure 5.2 Components of competent leadership

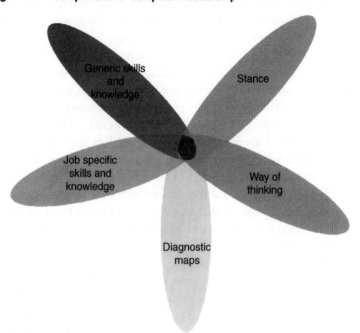

However, in order to appropriately use these skills and this knowledge, they have to possess the stance and way of thinking discussed above. In many ways the most effective leaders of educational change are very similar in their stance and way of thinking to exemplary teachers of adults: the staff for whom they are responsible are their learners and the workplace is the classroom. Both focus on learning and learning is change. Successful change leaders are impressive, therefore, because of the way in which their stance, way of thinking, knowledge and skills operate in combination to propel group learning for collaborative change. As Farson (1996: 144) says, 'the real strength of a leader is the ability to elicit the strength of the group. This paradox is another way of saying that leadership is less the property of a person than the property of a group.'

This more comprehensive view of what is necessary for competent performance as a leader of change in education is depicted in Figure 5.2.

DEVELOPING EXPERTISE AS A CAREER-LONG LEARNER

It is clear that, given the constantly changing context of daily practice in education (see Chapter 1), what educators currently know and can do now, no matter how effective, will not necessarily remain relevant. That is, their professional learning cannot be 'one-off'. Instead it must be career long. In facing this challenge, people in every occupation, including education and training, have to become adept at doing two things. First, at identifying which aspects of their present practice require change, and second, for the areas for improvement identified, at figuring out how to most efficiently and effectively go about addressing and monitoring their learning of them.

Such ongoing professional learning requires continuous upgrading of both practitioners' expertise in their specific professional area and their skill as a leader, manager and teacher. It requires a stance, way of thinking and organisational milieu which support their engagement in relevant and efficient self-managed professional learning. That is, they must be capable not only at leading change with others but at managing their own personal ongoing professional change (learning).

Developing every individual's capacity for lifelong learning is now at the centre of the educational reform agenda of a number of governments.[9] Countries and organisations which are capable of ongoing reform, innovation and learning require individuals who are good at it too. There are some things which educators can do personally in order to meet this challenge. And there are some things which other people (especially administrators and policy makers) can do to help.

What educators can do individually

Educators are in a strategically important position to influence their students' capability and willingness to manage their own learning. As Fullan (1993: 145) points out:

> When teachers work on personal vision-building and see how their commitment to making a difference in the classroom is connected to the wider purpose of education, it gives practical and moral meaning to their profession. When they pursue learning through constant inquiry they are practising what they preach, benefiting themselves and their students by always learning.

The work of Alan Tough (1979) suggests that much significant adult learning is done without undertaking formal courses or staff development programs, that it occurs more personally, often using valued colleagues and friends rather than print as a primary resource. Tough's research indicates further that people consistently express dissatisfaction with their ability to carry out these self-managed learning projects efficiently and effectively. It seems that previous educational experiences ill-equip them to initiate and direct their own learning and that many people would welcome coaching on how to do this better.

Particularly useful self-managed professional learning tactics for educators include:

- Continuously seeking to identify gaps in their expertise by using the guidelines for effective leadership as outlined in this chapter and the frameworks of 'best practice' outlined in other chapters of the book.
- Using the learning contract method to ensure they give focus to any self-managed learning projects that emerge (Anderson et al., 1996).
- Talking regularly and openly about their work, the changes they are facing and what constitutes 'effective and desirable' practice in their area of education with a knowledgeable friend or learning partner (Robinson et al., 1985).
- Visiting competent colleagues—seeing them in action,

looking for approaches to program design, workplace operation and managing changes which appear effective. Working out why these tactics are impressive and discussing this with the people concerned. Working with colleagues using and reflecting on the strategies outlined in Chapters 2 to 4.

- Participating in electronic learning networks of educators. Increasing numbers of interactive web sites for educators are emerging. These provide very convenient opportunities to find out about successful practice elsewhere and to discuss ways of handling practical change problems in education. More generally, seeking to become strategically 'plugged in' to what is happening in their field not just locally but nationally and internationally.

- Experimenting personally with the strategies suggested in this book and evaluating the results.

- Initiating relevant workplace action research in the ways suggested in Chapter 4 in order to enhance their skills in thinking critically about practice with a view towards improving their expertise in the area.

- Learning how to use recent developments in information technology to locate information efficiently and how to effectively read and review research in the ways outlined in Chapter 4.

- Becoming more aware of what they do as they prepare for and seek to implement program or workplace innovations, using the frameworks discussed throughout the book, especially the profile of the effective change leader.

- Identifying and discussing with trusted colleagues how best to handle common change dilemmas.

- Identifying and evaluating their stance when such dilemmas arise. This could include comparing their stance with that outlined in this chapter. It should include, in particular, developing a willingness to face and learn from errors. As John Dewey (1933: 114) noted over 50 years ago, 'Nothing shows the trained thinker better than the use he makes of his errors and mistakes'.

- Reflecting on experience. Noticing what aspects of daily

practice are most disturbing and which ones are satisfying. Critically reflecting on how well these are handled.

- Identifying and evaluating their goals and priorities for education. This could include identifying and evaluating any preferences they have for particular education 'tribes' (see Chapter 2) and, more generally, considering their position on the various educational futures outlined in Chapter 6.

- Finding out from successful colleagues how they have gone about their informal as well as their formal professional learning—how they organise their time, priorities, how they get useful answers to questions quickly and conveniently.

The excellent book, *Beginning with Ourselves*, by David Hunt (1987) contains a large number of exercises which will help develop skills in many of the above areas.

What others can do to support educators' self-managed learning

As noted in Chapter 2 when discussing implementation support, it is now clear that the most effective approach to staff development is for the organisation to make it ongoing, multifaceted and change specific. As the Price Waterhouse Change Integration Team (1996: 225) found: 'Ten days of training per year is giving way to the concept of "every day as a development experience".'

A workplace which has a profile such as that outlined in Chapter 3 will encourage and support educators to engage in ongoing collaborative learning and improvement projects. A workplace which is unfocused, dominated by constant meetings and endless memoranda, a place which is unproductive, unenhancing and characterised by back-biting will have the opposite effect.

The attributes of a workplace which actively supports change-specific staff learning are listed below. They are summarised from the detailed discussion in Chapter 3. It is important to recognise how important these attributes are for organisational learning, success and survival. And, irrespective of their position, every member of staff can actively contribute to putting them into place.

- A collaborative culture and a supportive climate.
- Staff selection and development approaches that focus on the profile of the effective change manager outlined in this chapter.
- Effective leadership.
- Existence of ongoing individualised professional development and mentoring schemes.[10]
- Effective identification and dissemination of good practice.
- Efficient, focused communication systems and approaches.
- Administrative support directly linked to the service's core purpose of consistently developing and implementing quality learning programs.
- A structure which balances top-down and bottom-up decision making and makes the responsibilities of different staff in this process explicit.
- Continuous monitoring of all aspects of service operation with the view of continuously enhancing the quality of what happens.
- Efficient documentation and record-keeping practices.
- An ongoing strategic planning approach which doesn't get too bogged down in the production of long-winded planning documents.

All of this implies a quite fresh approach to and conception of what constitutes effective professional learning for educators.

> Staff development will never have its intended impact as long as it is grafted onto [places of learning] in the form of discrete, unconnected projects. The closer one gets to the culture of [these places] and the professional lives of teachers, the more complex and daunting the reform agenda becomes. More powerful strategies are needed for more powerful changes. (Fullan, 1990: 21)

Support for self-managed learning can be given in an even more fundamental way. As recent government reports highlight,[11] schools and post-secondary education institutions need to give far more explicit attention in their learning programs to the skills of self-managed learning. Quite simply it is of little use calling for people to engage in such self-direction if their prior educational experiences have ignored (and in some cases actually contradicted) its development.

CONCLUSION

There is little doubt that effective, sustainable change in education—whether it be program change, organisational change or personal change—does not just happen, it must be led. However, as this chapter has emphasised, leadership does not just fall to people in management positions—this is, in fact, a recurring misconception. As emphasised at the start of this chapter, everyone can be (and often is) a leader of change in their own area of expertise.

This chapter has emphasised that it is the stance (emotional intelligence) and 'contingent' way of thinking (cognitive intelligence) of leaders that makes the difference when change is in the air. Of course, their levels of experience, skills, knowledge and qualifications do play a part, but change leadership fails if the requisite stance and way of thinking are absent. This has profound implications for what should be highlighted in staff selection, promotion and development in education and how these activities should be approached.

If a critical mass of staff possess the stance and way of thinking profiled, then the education service they occupy will be well positioned to 'ride the waves of change' effectively. This is because the teams necessary to drive the change process require people who can work together productively and with focus. They require people who are capable and willing to take on leadership roles when needed.

It is through this approach that program and organisational change can be combined with the skills of individual professional learning to produce a 'learning organisation'. Like the successful teacher of adults, effective change leaders recognise that their role is to give focus to change and build the capacity of those involved to manage it.

In Chapter 1 it was suggested that educational organisations which fail to keep an eye on their external environment do so at their peril. It is upon the importance of looking outwards and forwards, not just inwards at current provision, that the final chapter concentrates.

6
—
LOOKING OUTWARDS
AND FORWARDS IN
EDUCATION

*The river you put your foot in today is not
the river you will put your foot in tomorrow.*

Chinese proverb

This chapter explores exactly why connecting with the external environment and keeping an eye on what lies 'down the track' for education is so important. As the Chinese proverb above implies, the context in which educators must operate is continuously moving, flexing and changing. To ignore what is happening beyond the local education centre is, therefore, both inefficient and perilous.

In this chapter the essentially inward focus of earlier chapters shifts to looking outwards. The importance of linking more systematically with the wider environment, using networks to identify best practice and new directions, and developing partnerships for improvement is discussed. In addition the importance of anticipating the future for education, both in your particular sector and more generally, as well as the external influences which must be monitored and some anticipated futures for the field are explored. The need to distinguish between 'change' and 'progress' as we look outwards and forwards in education is highlighted and the central role which values play in the change process is emphasised.

The general proposition put forward in this chapter then is that, if an education service is to sustain and continuously improve what it does, a close eye must be kept not only on the present and what is happening inside the service (see Chapters 2 to 5) but also on the future and what is going on outside it. Being too present oriented and inward looking may mean that the march of history passes by the school, college, training department or university. Equally, being too future oriented and outward looking may mean that nothing worthwhile is achieved in present practice. The chapter emphasises, therefore, that what is necessary for effective change management is striking the right balance between looking inside and outside, concentrating on the present and the future, and being both reactive and proactive.

LOOKING OUTWARDS: THE IMPORTANCE OF CONNECTING WITH THE WIDER ENVIRONMENT

Consider this proposition from Michael Fullan (1993: 38): 'Many organisations work hard on internal development but fail to keep a proactive learning stance towards the environment. This fatal flaw is as old as evolution.'

What Fullan is saying here is vitally important for a number of reasons since education providers cannot and should not operate in isolation from the society of which they are part. Their funding comes from external sources. They are ultimately influenced by the government and private sector policies which determine how such funding is to be distributed. Knowing what these policy agendas are, how they might be changing and attempting to influence their shape are all important reasons for looking outwards.

There are many people and groups in the wider community from which an education service can learn. There are colleagues in other locations who are already further down the path upon which the local centre is moving and who can, because of this, reduce the time wasted in 'reinventing the wheel'. There are professional organisations, employers and policy advisers who are an important source of change ideas. There are community service organisations, government departments and relevant companies with whom mutually beneficial partnerships for learning or research can be formed.

As Fullan (1993: 39) emphasises:

> There are far more ideas 'out there' than 'in here' . . . Successful organisations have many antennae to tap into and to contribute to the demands of change which are constantly churning in the environment. They treat the internal and external milieu with equal respect. Seeing 'our connectedness to the world' and helping others to see it is a moral purpose and a teaching/learning opportunity of the highest order.

Using networks to identify best practice

As noted when discussing strategic networking and benchmarking in Chapter 3:

> One of the major challenges facing managers is avoiding becoming 'bogged down' in the internal issues of their organisations. Retaining or developing sufficient perspective on the external environment is essential in order to make sense of the internal issues . . . The external environment should be a source of opportunities, challenges and triggers for new ideas and ways of thinking and behaving . . .
>
> It is important to study best practice elsewhere—not in order to copy but to learn about yourself. (Binney & Williams, 1995: 88–9, 160)

The importance of 'being plugged in' to educators' professional networks has been emphasised continuously throughout this book. One of the best sources for ideas on what does or does not work best are fellow educators who are further advanced in dealing with common problems. This is as true for the process of learning program design (see Chapter 2) as it is for the process of workplace improvement (see Chapter 3), workplace action research (see Chapter 4) or the development of individual professional competence (see Chapter 5). Quite simply, operating in isolation is never as effective as working collaboratively, provided the people involved have the experience, stance and way of thinking necessary to add practical value to change project at hand.

The development of strategically useful contacts with people across the city, country and the world is being made increasingly easy through the Internet. There are formal web sites around many of the current changes taking place in education and training. There are also less formal chat groups emerging. The art in using these developments is to identify which networks are worth participating in and which are not. Holding seminars and workshops and participating in key conferences can also be ways of expanding a network of contacts. So too can enrolling in well respected development programs and university courses where 'rising stars' are known to get involved.

Using external partnerships for improvement

A particularly powerful form of networking involves the development of partnerships for improvement. These partnerships have the benefit of enhancing the quality of key aspects of a local school, college, university or training program. They involve two or more partners bringing together their unique expertise and resources to work on a common development priority. This is an excellent example of how different bodies and groups can work together for mutual benefit, how they can complement each other and avoid the duplication of functions or resources. It is an example of the sort of collaboration at an external level, which was advocated at an internal level in Chapter 3.

The following three case studies are examples of productive partnerships between organisations for a range of educational purposes.

Professional education

In a Graduate Certificate in Diabetes Education and Management, two faculties at the University of Technology, Sydney (Education and Nursing) and two leading Australian Diabetes

Education Centres (one operating out of Royal North Shore Hospital and the other out of St Vincent's Hospital, both in Sydney) joined forces to design and deliver the program. The course operates in mixed mode, caters for diabetes educators across Australia and New Zealand and features a wide range of work-based learning and research projects.

Each of these institutions could have offered their own course in diabetes education and management. However, by sharing each other's facilities and expertise and offering a combined course, the quality of the learning program and the benefits to the participants were increased many-fold. The case study is documented and discussed in detail in Scott (1996c).

Innovative links program in school education

With the support of the National Schools Network, staff and students from the School of Teacher Education at the University of Technology, Sydney worked in partnership with staff from a number of surrounding primary and secondary schools. Using the action research process outlined in Chapter 4 a number of specific improvement priorities for each school were identified and addressed. The schools benefited from having access to the time, expertise and resources of the university, the university benefited from having its staff and students grapple with real life change situations. A detailed evaluation of the program is included in Scott et al. (1996).

Workplace learning partnership program

The National Centre for Workplace Learning Partnerships at Middlesex University in the UK links the research and learning resources of the entire university to the workplace learning needs of the staff in partner companies. Staff development and workplace change are directly linked to university credit using a series of workplace studies awards ranging from certificates and diplomas to masters and doctorates. Learning programs are custom tailored to the needs of the individual, the company and the award requirements of the university. All awards include a workplace action research project and participants receive advanced standing for their current competence where these meet the requirements of an agreed capability framework. For further details see the National Centre's home page: http://www.mdx.ac.uk/www/ncwblp/

Connecting with relevant professional organisations

There are numerous local, national and international professional organisations available for educators. In Australia, for example, they range from subject-specific organisations (like an English Teachers Association), sector-specific unions (for example, the TAFE Teachers Association), innovation-specific groups (for instance, the Australian Problem Based Learning Consortium) to peak bodies like the Australian College of Education, the Australian Council for Adult Literacy, the Australian Institute for Training and Development, the Higher Education Research and Development Association or the Australian Association for Adult and Community Education. International groups include organisations like the Technology Roundtable run by the American Association for Higher Education.

Such groups can, if judiciously selected, provide valuable networking opportunities and up-to-date information on current developments, conferences and the publications available in the professional area(s) covered.

LOOKING FORWARDS: THE IMPORTANCE OF ANTICIPATING WHAT THE FUTURE HOLDS FOR EDUCATION

Not only are the most effective educational institutions 'plugged into' their present environment, responding to and contributing to the issues and needs of the day, they also look forwards. This is done in recognition of the age-old truism that 'the only thing that is permanent is change' (Heraclitus, 500 BC). This does not, however, mean that they necessarily involve themselves in longwinded, repetitive 'visioning' exercises. Rather it entails making sure they are plugged into the networks best positioned to sense what waves of change may be approaching.

This notion of 'strategic networking' involves being in ongoing contact (either directly or indirectly through a professional association) with groups close to those who shape the research and political agendas in education and those who control funding. Looking forwards is as necessary as looking outward. It ensures that the institution is well positioned to handle 'the inevitable waves of change' when they arrive.

External influences to keep an eye on

The following external sources of change were first identified in Chapter 1. In looking forwards it is important to understand the ways in which alterations in these factors may have a profound impact on an education service. Consider, for example, the way in which recent movements in each of the areas identified below have already had or will have an impact on your education service.

- Governments change and, when this happens, a shift in priorities concerning education is likely. For example, funding priorities may change, new structures or policies may be introduced, old initiatives may be defunded, new groups, content or approaches to learning can be given priority.
- New technological developments can emerge which can have direct implications for the content of educational programs or open up new possibilities for their design and delivery. Consider, for example, the dramatic influence which current developments in information technology are having on education.
- Economic conditions can change and this can trigger changes in overall levels of government and industry funding for education, in employment patterns and in the funding balance between different sectors of education.
- The attitudes and expectations of learners can change as general social values, attitudes and expectations change.

178

- Demographic changes can result in an education service having to cater for quite new sorts of clients.
- The organisation of which an individual's particular service is part can change—its policy directions can alter, it can be restructured, its senior management can move on. Each of these events can have profound implications for local players.

Adult literacy hypothetical

Reprinted below is the script of a hypothetical[1] run before a live audience of 200 educators at the Australian Council for Adult Literacy's 20th Annual Conference.

In the hypothetical, educational practitioners play a role similar to their own, adopting a new name to allow them to separate their real life persona from what they say. They are always cast into a fictional institution very similar to their real life one. As the hypothetical unfolds they are asked to respond to a series of unexpected challenges and perplexing situations embedded in a fictional story. These dilemmas are identified by detailed prior research with practitioners in the educational sector under consideration.

The aim of the hypothetical is to highlight these key change dilemmas and the futures for education of which they are indicative. In witnessing colleagues attempting to address them, observers are caused to reflect on what their position is in relation to these futures and on what they would do if confronted by them.

As you read through the script below reflect on what you would say or do if you were the characters involved. Consider how many of the dilemmas raised are currently being faced or are likely to unfold for your sector of education in the coming years. A film of what the players said in response to the hypothetical is available through Australia's Summer Hill Films.[2]

We start our story at Central College—a place we first visited some twelve years ago. Times have changed at Central since then. In those days funding for adult literacy was more readily available, staff numbers and enrolments were increasing and the majority of teaching and learning was done in the college. Now there are cuts to funding, many other competing organisations have entered the field, staff are having to get involved in competitive tendering, more and more literacy teaching must be delivered in the workplace and there generally seems to be greater scrutiny of what is happening.

At Central we have Chris who is the College's Head of Literacy and an experienced campaigner. We have a number of full-time staff like Anne and many part-timers like Sally.

Chris, you have just been called by the principal. Head Office has told her that, with these recent budget cuts, some programs must go. She wants you to justify why your literacy programs should stay in preference to the many trade programs run by Central. You decide to meet with Anne and Sally to work out what to do. Could you please have your meeting now.

(They have their meeting.)

During your meeting the principal suddenly appears at the door. She is holding a copy of the *Morning Clarion* in her hands. The headlines on the front page scream out 'Six million still can't read and write: Minister demands answers'. The article is written by that doyen of the press Hopwood Jackson. The principal says Hopwood is claiming that the millions invested in adult literacy since the 1980s appear to have been squandered, and is quoting recent studies which indicate that up to 50 per cent of the unemployed have substandard literacy and numeracy skills. The principal is clearly unimpressed. Sure enough, despite all your arguments, she recommends the next week that some literacy programs will have to be cut.

Sally, these program cuts will probably mean that, as a part-timer, you will be the first to go. How do you feel? *(She answers.)* Some people are suggesting that one way to save jobs like yours is to put everyone on contract. Sally, do you support such an idea? *(She answers.)* Anne, what about you as a full-timer with permanency—would you support this? After all, it will keep Sally in work and she does have three kids to feed. *(She answers.)*

The Minister responds. The government announces the establishment of what becomes known as the East Review. This review is to be undertaken by Dr East, a quality assurance expert who has just completed similar hard hitting reviews in two overseas countries. His brief is to establish why the country still has six million people with poor literacy skills, to find out if there has been any featherbedding and to advise the Minister on the most cost-efficient course of action.

Hopwood Jackson is clearly delighted with this development and runs a long article in the *Clarion* praising the government for finally getting tough on the fluffiness that has been allowed to creep into areas of education like adult literacy.

Chris, Anne and Sally, it really does look like job losses are on the cards, doesn't it? But wait, just when all seems lost, Chris, you get a phone call from that well known multinational company Skull Chemicals. It is the Head of HRD on the line and he says he's heard of your work in workplace literacy, especially what a good job one of your part-time teachers, Sally, has been doing. He wants to invite you to tender for a workplace literacy training program which could be worth hundreds of thousands of dollars. This will guarantee jobs for all if you win the contract. Chris, will you tender?

(She answers.) Will you still tender if you hear that there have been international demonstrations against Skull's environmental safeguards' record? *(She answers.)* What about if you hear that, in their Asian operations, they use indebted families as low cost labour in their factories? *(She answers.)*

Over at the National Centre for Industry Training Quality, Karen is watching developments closely.

Karen, how are your industry colleagues reacting to the establishment of the East Review and the sorts of revelations being made by Hopwood Jackson? *(She answers.)*

Well, Karen, Hopwood himself calls you. He's heard you have your finger on the pulse when it comes to the industry view of training. He wants to check if some of the reactions he has been getting from his industry contacts are more widespread. He's heard, for example, that current providers of workplace literacy just don't deliver relevant programs, that what industry wants is more train-the-trainer and less of these middle-class teachers coming in every once and a while and running off-the-job classes. Is he right? *(She answers.)*

Hopwood is impressed with your answers. So it's not long before you get a call from Dr East's office wanting to set up a meeting. You agree and receive a briefing note from Dr East saying that he wants to get your reactions to a few ideas that he has been playing around with. These involve the idea of introducing screening tests in literacy for all new employees. This will enable companies to save considerable amounts of money by not having to run workplace literacy programs and will, therefore, increase productivity and profitability. You'll support this won't you? *(She answers.)*

Penny, as a key player in the National Union for Post-Secondary Teachers you are actively looking at how best to handle what is happening with your comrades. Penny, how does the Union feel about the way things are going? *(She answers.)*

You hear that the Minister is considering the introduction of a national hot line for users of adult literacy services to express their satisfaction with the current quality of the service they are receiving. Isn't this an ideal opportunity to show Hopwood and East—by the positive response you'd know you'll get—that your highly trained teachers are of top quality and that the level of customer satisfaction is high? *(She answers.)*

Penny, another issue is emerging. You hear that in some parts of the country private providers are employing staff at non-union rates. These providers argue that this will give more people jobs. Isn't there something in this argument, especially in a period where there are more trained teachers than there are jobs, when there are such high rates of unemployment? *(She answers.)*

As we know, in recent years, Central College has been joined by many other providers who also bid for adult literacy projects. These include SkillShape, whose manager is Jane, and Western Adult Education Centre, whose principal is Richard.

Jane, SkillShape has fallen on hard times as the government has increasingly withdrawn funding from training projects for the unemployed. Will you be going for the Skull job? *(She answers.)* Richard, you are a well known humanist. You won't be bidding, will you? *(He answers.)*

We all know that to win all of these literacy training contracts it helps if you have the lowest per unit cost. Richard, how can you achieve this and still maintain quality? *(He answers.)*

Something very exciting happens. You are both approached in confidence to see if you are interested in getting involved in an I.T.-based literacy project being developed at the National Technology Park. A team, inspired by the groundbreaking work of Chuck Silicon in the States, has been working on an innovation which they call Cyberliteracy. It is a fully interactive CD Rom that teaches reading and writing without the need for face-to-face teaching. Richard, this will cut those high staff costs. You have the opportunity to come in as a partner—what will you do? *(He answers.)* Jane, how will you assess the educational merit of such a development? *(She answers.)*

Meanwhile, Hopwood Jackson's newspaper campaign is gathering pace. He is now floating the idea that there should be national quality reviews of adult literacy and that what should happen is that most of the funding spent in past years on adult literacy should be shifted to primary schools.

At the State Ministry things are hotting up.

Maria, you are the State Minister's senior policy adviser. He is getting furious about all this negative press. And it now looks like Roy Morton's highly popular TV current affairs program *Day in Review* is going to run a series. Maria, the Minister wants your suggestions on damage control. What do you advise? *(She answers.)*

Maria, both you and John, the president of the National Adult Literacy Council, get a leaked copy of Dr East's recommendations. *(These are handed to Maria and John and read out to the audience.)* Dr East's recommendations are as follows:

1 Adult literacy should become more self-funding with an increased focus on train-the-trainer in industry.
2 Community classes for the unemployed should be cut.
3 There should be further casualisation of the adult literacy workforce. This will make teaching more

cost-efficient, market-driven and, because there will be less on-costs, provide a greater spread of employment opportunity for trained teachers.

4 The majority of funding should now be shifted to lifting the quality of primary school literacy and numeracy programs.

5 Significant investment should be put into the Cyberliteracy project as part of this initiative.

Maria and John, you decide to meet over a cappuccino to discuss what these recommendations mean and how you will handle them. Please have your meeting now. *(They have their meeting.)*

During the meeting your mobile rings, John. It's the executive producer of *Day in Review*. They are running a series called 'Falling standards and soft cops in education' and you are invited to come on the program. You accept.

The day of the program arrives. You are on set and the *Day in Review* program has just gone live to air. Roy Morton is saying:

'Tonight we are seeking answers from the President of the National Adult Literacy Council to the questions all the country is asking. These questions are:

'First, how come, with the millions the taxpayer has spent on adult literacy over the past decade, we've still got six million people who can't read and write properly in this country?

'And second, could you please tell us why we shouldn't act on what it looks like Dr East will be recommending—things like *(he reads the leaked recommendations).*

'John, what do you say? Time is short so be brief.' *(He answers.)*

Suddenly, the presenter interrupts you, John. He says:

'We've got exciting news. Dr East has been listening

to what is happening in another city. We've organised a live cross to him for his reaction. Dr East?' *(The lights dim and a large screen descends. As it does Dr East, played by an actor, appears. He is fiddling with his earpiece and apparently unaware he is on camera. He is saying to someone off camera: 'What a pack of rubbish.' Then, alerted to the fact that he is on air, he looks to the camera and starts talking.)*

'Thank you. I have been listening to what has been going on and frankly I am worried about what I'm hearing. Let me start off by saying that I am concerned to hear that there have been leaks of my recommendations to the Minister and the Federal Police will be invesigating. Let me also say that some tough decisions have to be made and I know Minister Sharp will make them.' *(He then goes over his recommendations.)*

'I would like your viewers to understand that my recommendations have not been pulled out of the air. They are based on the twin foundations of human capital theory and the need for integrated literacy. Let me explain. In terms of human capital theory I believe that we must introduce screening tests so that only those who can read, write and calculate properly get employed from now on. Human capital theory says that this will motivate those unemployed who can't meet our standards to pay to get these skills in order to get a job.

'As to those workers who are already employed but lack the literacy and numeracy skills required, I believe we should adopt an integrated literacy approach. What does this mean? It means that we should be training the workplace supervisors to teach literacy as a normal part of the job, not having people who have little understanding of the world of work swanning in once or twice a week.

'The savings we will make will be put into our

primary schools, into the young people who will be the future of this country. We can't afford to put money into the unemployed, into people who have already failed. We just don't have the resources. And . . .' *(Suddenly the screen goes blank and the lights go up.)*

'Unfortunately', says Roy Morton, 'we seem to have lost our link.'

At home, everyone has been watching the program. Chris, Anne and Sally—what is going through your minds as you watch the program? What do you think the future holds? Richard, Penny? Jane? Maria? Karen? *(They answer in turn.)*

Well, so ends our story. Of course, all of this is totally hypothetical—none of what we have discussed tonight is likely to occur . . . is it? If we were to run another hypothetical in ten years—let's say in 2009—do you think there will still be an adult literacy movement in this country? If there is, will it look like it does today? What will be the hot themes and dilemmas then? How about we meet in 2009 to see?

Change versus progress

As emphasised in Chapter 1 and as the above hypothetical demonstrates, the change process in education is particularly value-laden and subjective. Everyone upon whom a particular change project has an impact is constantly making judgments about the worth of what is unfolding. Fullan (1991: 15) puts the issue as follows:

> Change for the sake of change will not help. New programs either make no difference, help improve the situation or make it worse. The difference between change and progress can be most forcefully brought home if we ask: What if the majority of educational changes . . . actually made matters

worse, however unintentionally, than if nothing had been done?

There is, therefore, a profound difference between educational change (the objective fact of something becoming different) and progress (a subjective judgment by particular individuals that a specific change has been in a direction which they deem desirable). Educators, as we have seen in Chapters 2 and 3, constantly make judgments about what changes are worthwhile and which ones are not.

It is vitally important, therefore, to be clear on one's own educational values and to keep these in mind as each new wave of change comes along. In some cases individuals will embrace a particular change, in others they will not. Either way it is crucial as a change leader (see Chapter 5) to be aware of one's own assumptions and values and to be prepared to stand up for these principles when prospective changes are discussed. Handy (1995: 18) suggests the necessary mindset:

> Life will never be easy, nor perfectible, nor completely predictable. It will be best understood backwards, but we have to live it forwards. To make it livable . . . we have to learn to use the paradoxes, to balance the contradictions and the inconsistencies and to use them as an invitation to find a better way.

Some likely futures for education

Below, a series of propositions about the directions for education in the twenty-first century are put forward. Which are most or least important to you and why? What does this reveal about your educational values and assumptions? Which do you believe are most or least likely to occur irrespective of your personal position in relation to them? Are there futures you can see which are missing?

Your position on likely futures for education

1 Education will focus far more on developing a capability to manage continuous change collaboratively. Consider,

for example, Michael Fullan's (1993: 136) proposition in his book *Change Forces*:

We know increasingly more about what learning should focus on, and how people learn. The necessary combination of intellectual development ('education for understanding') and social development (such as cooperative learning's emphasis on learning to work in groups) is becoming more evident. The abilities to think and present ideas on the one hand, and to work with others on the other hand are being recognised by education and businesses alike as central to the world's future. Permeating these twin purposes is a third purpose—the positive disposition to keep on learning in the face of constant change and societal complexity. Put another way, the ability to cope with change, learning as much as possible with each encounter is the generic capacity needed for the twenty-first century.

Or the conclusions of Candy et al. (1994: 44):

Thriving, not merely surviving, in [a situation] where change is a constant and ever-present challenge—not an occasional disruptive occurrence—is the most obvious sign of our lifelong learner. Not only does she possess the skills and knowledge to operate effectively and efficiently in this environment, she also has the creativity, intuition, and motivation to view this challenging environment as a vehicle for her own self-improvement. Our lifelong learner stands out from those who have similar skills and knowledge, and even the desire to learn, because she is able to strategically manage her own learning.

2 Education, including school education, will become more vocationally oriented.
3 Education will give far more emphasis to individual needs, ethics, attitudes and creativity, and be less of a training treadmill. Consider the following passage from *Redesigning Education* by Wilson and Daviss (1994: 9–10, 13):

In the industrial age—roughly from the 1870s through the 1950s—national wealth was rooted in an abundance of raw materials and a steady supply of factory labor, and the

conventional structure of . . . education was well matched to
society's needs. Most students learned, through rote exercises,
to read and do simple mathematics; all learned to memorise
information and follow instructions . . . schooling still bears
the stamp of the antiquated, quantity-based economy that it
was organised to serve. Students move through courses and
grades at a fixed pace, like products moving along an
assembly line that can't be slowed down long enough to
remedy the flawed processes that inevitably lead to flawed
products . . . In most classrooms today students' chairs still
face the teacher, just as they have for more than a century.
The teacher delivers the information; [students] receive it.
Teachers ask questions; [students] answer when called upon.
For most of the rest of their class time, far too many students
work silently and alone at their desks performing rote
exercises. Their progress is measured in letter grades, which
[they] win at one another's expense . . . [It] is one of the
few places where citizens in George Washington's America
would feel right at home.

4 There will be far greater linking and cooperation and less
  discontinuity between different sectors of education. This
  proposition is hardly new. For example, in the 1930s John
  Dewey (1930, 1933) emphasised that it was of little use
  to put effort into the reform of higher education if the
  foundations at the elementary and secondary levels were
  weak. In this scenario, competition between different institutions and sectors in education will become a thing of
  the past.
5 Access and equity will be essential goals for education in
  the twenty-first century. Disadvantaged groups will be
  given positive support to access and succeed in higher
  levels of education. New developments in information
  technology (for example, uses of Internet-based learning)
  will assist people disadvantaged by distance to participate
  more fully in these opportunities.
6 The assessment systems in education, especially end of high
  school examinations, will have been radically revised to
  ensure that they more explicitly tap capabilities like critical
  thinking, creativity, the ability to get to the core of a

perplexing issue and the ability to manage change. This shift in assessment emphasis will have encouraged the redesign of learning programs so that they more directly develop them. Wilson and Daviss (1994: 177–9), citing Gardner (1991: 154), explain the situation as follows:

'Students may learn to give "proper" interpretations of historical events or "proper" readings of classic novels or plays when they are under the guidance of a teacher . . . They can adopt subtle [learning strategies] that will help them succeed in formal examinations. But when they are asked about the same types of events or characters some time later, they may well regress to the earlier more entrenched and more stereotypical ways of interpreting human behaviour.' For example, people may learn as students that World War I was caused by a confluence of complex events that culminated in the assassination of Archduke Ferdinand . . . But the same people might unconsciously attribute the cause of a race riot in Los Angeles to the jury's verdict in a single-police brutality case . . .

Schools intent on seeing students master higher-order skills must explicitly confront and destroy the simplistic intuitive theories that linger from childhood.

7 The single discipline focus which currently dominates education will have been replaced by learning systems which are cross–disciplinary. In doing this the emphasis will be on the consideration of the really substantive issues facing our society like environmental degradation, poverty, population growth and how to develop sustainable futures, issues which can only be understood by concurrently viewing them from multiple perspectives, for example, by simultaneous reference to philosophy, economics, science, technology, literature and history.

8 There will be far more two–way internationalisation of education. That is, there will be far more opportunity for local students to study overseas and vice versa. Courses from prestigious overseas institutions will be available on the Internet and will be open to local students, even if

this results in a drop in enrolments and funding available for local institutions.

9 There will be far more flexibility in the design and delivery of learning programs. Whenever feasible, learning at all levels will have multiple entry and exit points, more flexible rates of progression and learning pathways. Learning programs will be better tailored to the needs of the individual, new technologies will be appropriately used to make learning more convenient and self-directed. Boud and Feletti (1991: 23–4) predict that change:

will make self-directed learning throughout their life a sine qua non . . . Adapting to and participating in change and self-directed learning are composite competencies. Each will require the development of a number of component competencies, such as the skills of communication, critical reasoning, a logical and analytical approach to problems, reasoned decision making and self evaluation.

10 Educational organisations and workplaces will have become learning organisations, places which model and practise a capability to manage continuous quality improvement and innovation efficiently and effectively. Collaborative cultures and partnerships within and beyond the organisation will be a distinctive attribute of such places. Teacher education institutions will be at the forefront of this development.

11 A capability to work collaboratively in teams will be a core focus for education, as suggested by Wilson and Daviss (1994: 185):

Clearly, cooperative learning's success carries implications beyond school. More and more adult workers find themselves in teams, working together to identify and solve problems and accomplish mutual goals. Solutions to social problems—achieving racial and gender equity, resolving tensions between industrial needs and environmental protection, strengthening families—increasingly demand the same kinds of group-oriented, cooperative skills.

12 There will be increasing pressure for education, especially at the post-secondary level, to become a fully user-pays system.

It is vitally important in conclusion to remind you of the 'what' and 'why' of change. Although this book has concentrated on the 'how' of change in education, it is clearly the combination of these questions that makes the difference. No change effort is ever value free. After all, Hitler was eminently effective as a change manager and as Will Rogers (cited in Sherrin, 1995) put it: 'You can't say civilisation don't advance, however, for in every war they kill you in a new way.'

CONCLUSION

This chapter has demonstrated that, if an education service is to remain relevant, it must be consistently 'plugged into' what is happening beyond its walls. With the globalisation of many facets of life, including education, this imperative no longer applies just to an institution's region, state, province or even its country. Furthermore, by looking outwards, educators can help minimise a tendency towards 'groupthink' and 'balkanisation' in their organisations (see Chapter 2).

However, looking outwards cannot be an unfocused process in which people hope that by randomly visiting other locations, participating in conferences, surfing the Internet and so on, they might uncover something of interest. To be efficient it must be strategic. Staff who engage in external networking, benchmarking or site visits must know why they are undertaking these activities and be clear on how what they are seeking to learn will add value to daily practice back inside their institution. And this requires explicit coordination and leadership.

Just as the paradoxical nature of effective change management in education has been demonstrated in earlier chapters— for example, the importance of adopting strategies which are both top-down and bottom-up; of involving both teaching and administrative staff; of balancing stability with change, enhancement with innovation and pan-institutional with local developments; and of listening and leading—so too in this chapter the importance of looking both outside and inside with purpose has been reinforced. In each case it has been argued that it is the ability to appropriately balance both poles of the paradox that is most telling.

Equally, if an education service is to flourish, it must look simultaneously at both its present situation and the future. There are numerous scenarios on how education might unfold in the coming years included in the latter part of this chapter. Each demonstrates the key role which value judgment plays in every change project, and how there is a profound difference, therefore, between 'change' and 'progress'. It is appropriate to now conclude by emphasising that effective change management is not some sort of mechanistic process but a highly subjective, emotion-rich, human one. It is indeed true that change is learning and learning is change, and that values, motives, evaluation and human relationships underpin all that happens in it.

CONCLUSION

> *It is not as if we can avoid change, since it pursues
> us in every way. We might as well, then, make the best
> of it. The answer is not in avoiding change, but in turning
> the tables by facing it head on. The new mindset is to
> exploit change before it victimises us . . . . We can learn to
> reject unwanted change more effectively, while at the same
> time becoming more effective at accomplishing desired
> improvements. Grappling with educational change in
> self-defeating ways has been the modal experience over
> the last 30 years.*
>
> Michael Fullan (1991)

There is little doubt that every sector of education from early childhood to higher, further and adult education is in for a rough ride in the coming years.

This book has been written with this in mind. It does not, however, see such a situation as necessarily constituting a cause for despair. Instead, given what we now know about effective change management in education there is, indeed, some justification for optimism.

The book's perspective is that continuous change is inevitable and that the best tactic, as Fullan suggests, is to face it head on but to do so in an informed fashion. Challenges and futures like those outlined in Chapter 6 can be handled positively; educators can play an active role in ensuring education has a desirable impact, provided they come to grips with the real meaning of educational change and the most constructive ways of handling it as identified throughout the book. The approaches advocated have not emerged from a purely theoretical analysis of change but from the practical experience of hundreds of educators in different countries who believe they can make a difference and have learned how to manage the process effectively, efficiently and with purpose.

We have repeatedly found that, once they come to see the bigger picture and understand how the many pieces which make up the change puzzle are connected, educators feel less the victims of powerful and mysterious forces and more confident about what to do when change is in the air. This book has sought to develop this confidence and also to provide the tools which will enable educators to act on it. It is in this way that they can be enabled, as Fullan advocates, to turn the tables on change. Rather than always being on the back foot, it is anticipated that the book will help educators to shift their weight onto the front foot and to start leaning into the future with purpose and focus (Binney & Williams, 1995) and that it will also help them to gradually recognise problems as their friends (Fullan, 1993). Confidence and optimism in the face of relentless change do not arise spontaneously. They develop when people are explicitly assisted to make sense of what is happening and to figure out what to do about it.

This book argues for a close and consistent link between learning program change and workplace change in education. The need for these to go hand in hand is often not clearly recognised. Yet, if educational organisations fail to address these twin foundations of effective, ongoing quality improvement and innovation they cannot hope to remain relevant to the learners and societies they serve.

It is now more widely understood that the people who make up an organisation are its greatest asset. As Bullock (1985: 194) argues:

> [T]he greatest resources available to any organisation are the
> human ingenuity, experience and loyalty it can draw on.
> None are more commonly undervalued. Yet any investment
> put into tapping these by education (education far more than
> training), by securing active participation and with it the
> commitment of those working in any enterprise to its success
> will produce far greater returns than piling up investment in
> sites, buildings and equipment.

Such a proposition holds as well for an entire society as it
does for the institutions, communities and groups which make
it up. As Bullock suggests, it is primarily through education
that the capability to respond positively, creatively and effectively to inevitable change can be built. It is an odd paradox,
therefore, that although governments might agree with such
views in theory, in practice many of them appear to treat
education as if it were a cost rather than an investment.

There is emerging evidence (Putnam, 1993; Cox, 1995)
that whole communities which have learned to work collaboratively around focused development priorities and which
understand how to manage these changes efficiently and
effectively are far more successful in achieving their goals than
those characterised by competitiveness, blame, exclusiveness,
'white-anting' and derision. The very values which Putnam
and Cox identify at the societal level have been identified in
the research on effective change in educational institutions
reviewed throughout this book.

What then are these recurring values?[1] They are that:

- People can make a difference.
- Working together leads to a better outcome than working
  alone. However, being alone when it is appropriate is also
  important.
- How you treat people to a large measure explains how
  they treat you.
- Actions speak louder than words. Leading by example is
  a key ingredient in effective change management.
- People respond positively if given justified praise for
  changes achieved.

- A sense of humour indicates a sound perspective on the human condition.
- Listen authentically and learn. A responsive mindset is a key starting point to effective change.
- Recognise, tolerate and work with the fact that different people will bring with them different expectations of what constitutes progress and success.
- Taking a hard decision is sometimes essential and this requires courage.
- A willingness to take sensible risks is necessary if change is to succeed.
- All worthwhile change requires perseverence. Losing your cool, giving up too readily and over-reacting when things go wrong all short-circuit change.
- Accept that nothing ever goes exactly to plan.
- Facing and learning from your errors is to be admired.
- Manipulating, using and deceiving people, denigrating them behind their back, allocating blame and denying responsibility do not ultimately pay off.
- Denial is the enemy of progress.
- Forcing your ideas on others does not result in successful change.
- Expecting people new to a change to quickly grasp what its proponent may have spent months thinking through is unfair.

Such values are hardly new. They emerge whenever the stance of effective change leaders is identified (see Chapter 5). More generally, they underpin the humanist tradition in the west:

> Throughout these [past] 600 years, the humanist tradition has represented a refusal to accept a determinist or a reductionist view of man, an insistence that in some measure men and women, if they do not enjoy complete freedom, none the less have it in their hands to make choices . . . I submit that this is the continuing attraction of the humanist approach. (Bullock, 1985: 194, 197)

In practising such values and by adopting the approaches to managing change in education upon which they are built, educators will achieve a double pay-off. Not only will they optimise the chances that their desired changes will succeed and be sustained, they will also be modelling to their learners and colleagues the values central to a truly civil society.

Understanding and achieving successful change in education and training does indeed matter. It matters because relentless change in every sector of education is inevitable; it matters because the pressures for continuous change are increasing not decreasing; it matters because failed change brings with it not just economic but significant psychological and social costs; and it matters because how well we manage educational change right now will, in large part, determine the directions which broader societal changes take in the twenty-first century.

Teachers, lecturers, tutors, trainers and educational managers can indeed make a difference when change is in the air, provided they attend not just to what might change but to how their ideas for reform can be successfully translated into daily practice. It is the combination of the what *and* the how of change that will ultimately make the difference.

GLOSSARY

Accreditation The process of determining the educational worth of a learning module, course or provider, usually with the purpose of maintaining some general standard.

Articulation The process by which the successful completion of a course of study by a person is acknowledged if the person undertakes a further course of study in the same or another institution.

Assessment The act of gathering data about the attitudes, performance, knowledge or way of thinking of specific groups for use in evaluation (see also Field, 1990: 74–6, 197ff).

Capability Combination of attributes, qualities, skills and knowledge that enables a person to perform to a high standard in a given context and role.

Change The act of making different, of altering some aspect(s) of teacher education practice with (presumably) the purpose of improving the quality of service delivered to clients, especially students. This transitive definition of the term can be distinguished from the intransitive definition which sees 'change' as just 'happening' through a process of 'drift' and the action of forces not amenable to the influence of individuals. The term is distinguished from 'progress'.

Climate The level of morale at a place of work. Climate is more volatile than culture. Climate is concerned with current feelings and attitudes to the workplace; culture is more enduring and concerned with established ways of behaving.

Community education Education which tends to be needs-based and not for credit or part of a formal qualification.

Competence A competent person has the attributes necessary for task performance to the appropriate standards. These attributes include knowledge, cognitive abilities, skills and attitudes. This definition includes, therefore, three key elements: (i) attributes, (ii) performance, and (iii) standards (see Gonczi, 1992). An illustration of how this definition can be applied to the definition of manager competence in vocational education and training is given in Chapter 5 of this book.

Competency A combination of attributes underlying some aspect of successful professional performance. Relatively specific combinations of attributes are specific (or simple) competencies. Higher order competencies are relatively complex combinations of attributes (for example, judgment or posing questions), skills (for example, interpersonal) and attitudes (for example, patience or compassion) (see Gonczi, 1992).

Competency-based training A form of training that typically focuses on precise definitions of skills to be achieved to specified conditions and under specified standards. It can be used on or off the job. This more limited, behaviourist definition is gradually being replaced by competency-based education which concentrates on the development of all aspects of competence.

Conceptual framework A conceptual framework explains, either graphically or in narrative form, the main dimensions to be studied—the key factors or variables—and the presumed relationships amongst them (Miles & Huberman, 1984: 28).

Contingent thinking Ability to 'read' accurately what lies behind a perplexing situation and 'match' the most feasible and desirable response. A conditional way of thinking as distinct from a fixed or regurgitative one.

Continuation That phase of the change process which follows on after initiation and implementation. It can concern ensuring that the change continues to be supported and becomes built into standard operating procedures. More often that not it involves recycling through initiation and implementation as it becomes clear that the original innovation needs modification in the light of changing circumstances.

Culture The accepted and sought after ways of behaving in an organisation or workplace. This includes norms, predominant values, stance towards work and education, incentives and enduring interests.

Curriculum A term often used to describe a course of study. In this sense it can be seen as being interchangeable with the term 'learning program'. However, for many people, a 'curriculum' is associated with a pre-set and accredited course of study rather than one which is negotiated with the learner and open to ongoing modification.

Dilemma A dilemma requires a choice (often under considerable time pressure) between two or more potentially appropriate courses of action which set up a tension which must be resolved one way or the other (Huberman & Miles, 1984: 278).

Drift A process of change in VET which is unplanned and unsystematic (Hopkins, 1984).

Education A formal and systematic approach to supporting learning.

Enhancement A change in a current practice seen by those involved to have improved matters. A rise in quality.

Evaluation The process which leads to judgments about the worth, effectiveness and efficiency of an activity, project or strategy (McDonald & Bishop, 1990: 12). It can be formal or informal and can be formative (intended to improve that which is evaluated or summative (intended to sum up its overall benefit and impact).

Fidelity When used in relation to educational change
implies that 'users' should faithfully put into practice the
predetermined practices, content and procedures faithfully
to set standards.

Higher order competencies Relatively complex combinations of attributes (for example, judgment or posing
questions), skills (for example, interpersonal) and attitudes
(for example, patience or compassion) (see Gonczi, 1992).
Field (1990: 74) calls these 'under the surface' skills.

Impact The effect which a program or innovation has on
those intended to benefit from it or associated with it.
Impact is concerned with how the attitudes, knowledge
and skills of such people (or the groups and organisations
they occupy) actually change as a result of involvement in
the change effort.

Implementation 'The actual use of the innovation, or what
an innovation looks like in practice. This differs from both
intended and planned use' (Fullan & Pomfret, 1977: 340).
This would include activities like monitoring, adjusting
and supporting the change effort once underway. It is
distinguished from 'impact' which concerns the outcomes
of this effort.

Initiation Activities that occur when an innovatory idea is
first introduced. These might include assessing the readiness
for such an innovation, mobilisation of support, the development of a change plan and an implementation strategy,
formal adoption of the innovation and so on.

Innovate The process of making some structure, material,
or practice different.

Innovation An idea, practice or material *perceived* to be new
by the group or individual adopting it (Zaltman et al.,
1973). The focus here is on the perception whereas the
term change tends to look more at the objective reality—at
seeing if things are actually different.

Institutionalisation This concerns the attempt to build an
innovation into the standard operating procedures (such as
staffing and resourcing procedures) of an organisation. It
is misleading if it implies that the change will remain fixed

and that its support requirements will remain the same. Looking at institutionalisation is particularly important with innovations which have received on–off funding from some external body.

Knowledge Acquaintance with facts and principles in a particular branch of learning.

Learning Involves a change in attitudes, skills, knowledge and how we think. Learning is 'progressive' if the resulting behaviour and understanding of people is seen to be 'desirable'.

Learning culture A term used in attempts to create a workplace norm which values continuous reform improvement and learning how to do things better.

Learning goal The general outcome being sought in a learning program—goals vary with perspective. For some people a key goal is acquisition of knowledge and skills; for others it may be change in self-esteem or a different way of thinking.

Learning need 'Needs can be viewed as being a discrepancy between the present state of affairs and what is required' (Chappell, 1995).

Learning objective A learning objective is a specific change in attitude, skill, knowledge or way of thinking that helps achieve a learning goal.

Learning organisation An organisation which has developed the capability for continuous quality improvement and innovation.

Learning program A learning program is defined as a sequence of learning sessions that are developmental, linked and which meet the requirements of the learner and take into account the context in which the program is being delivered.

Loose coupling A phrase popularised by Wieck (1976) and conveys the message that although coupled events are responsive, each event preserves its own identity. The concept implies impermanence, dissolvability, all of which are potentially crucial properties of the glue that holds organisations together (Hopkins, 1984: 41).

Manage To bring about, succeed in accomplishing.

Mentor Someone (usually senior and well regarded) who can become a 'champion' for the innovation amongst the highest levels of the organisation.

Micropolitics The patterns of communications that occur in the 'hidden side of organisational life', the decisions concerning the innovation which are made in informal rather than formal settings (Ball, 1987; Hoyle, 1986).

Milieu An environment (such as a workplace), medium or condition.

Modules 'Self contained units of learning which can be completed individually or in a predefined sequence and which added together form a qualification' (Macken, 1989: ix).

Mutual adaptation A term invented by Berman and McLaughlin (1977) which refers to the fact that, as a change effort proceeds, the best tactic is to try, on the one hand, to modify the innovation to better fit the context in which it is being attempted and on the other hand try to modify the context to better accommodate the innovation.

Operators Seen to be a preferable term to 'users' as the latter implies a more passive role in the change process than is actually the case. An operator performs or runs an innovation effectively.

Paradox A paradox is a seemingly contradictory statement that may nonetheless be true (Price Waterhouse, 1996: 4). It is a technique commonly used in Zen Buddhist approaches to teaching and learning.

Performance skills A set of skills required to do a job to a set standard. They are acts which can be observed.

Progress A conclusion by specific individuals that a change has been in a desirable direction. Progress therefore involves evaluation, which, in turn involves a process of making value judgments.

Quality assurance Concentrates on the systematic introduction and monitoring of linked structures, processes and policies in order to achieve consistently high quality outcomes. Quality assurance should aim to support, monitor and assure the process of continuous quality improvement.

Quality assurance goes beyond quality control by extending the focus to prevention rather than post hoc analysis, from compliance with pre-set requirements to ongoing improvement and by concentrating not only on outcomes but improving the processes and structures that produce them. QA is concerned with building the organisation's ongoing capacity for effective change management.

Quality control A system that concentrates mainly on comparing outputs against set standards. It is a much more limited concept than quality assurance or quality improvement.

Quality improvement Continuous quality improvement and innovation should be a key outcome of an effective quality assurance system. The focus is the improvement in both outcomes and the structures, processes and policies necessary to achieve them.

Skill The ability to do something well.

Stance In the case of change management in VET, one's attitude towards work and the people involved in it. This is the affective dimension of professional competence.

Training A systematic approach which tends to focus more on the development of practical skills and knowledge in a set fashion than the development of 'higher order skills'.

Users In change management literature this tends to indicate a fidelity approach to change management where the people who are to put the innovation into practice are cast in a passive role. The art is to train these people to use the innovation 'correctly'.

Values Ideals, customs, standards of behaviour that evoke an emotional response for or against them in a given society or a given person.

Vocational education and training A systematic approach which focuses not only on practical skills and knowledge but on the development of higher order competencies as well. Adult VET refers to the use of this process with people beyond the compulsory school leaving age.

Way of thinking This is the cognitive dimension of professional competence and refers to the way in which people think about and think through what should be done at work. It involves how they go about problem construction as well as problem solving, how they think before, during and after action (Schön, 1983).

NOTES

Introduction

1 Price Waterhouse (1996).
2 See, for example, Barraclough et al. (1994), Candy et al. (1994), Feletti (1992), Gonczi et al. (1990), Gonczi (1994), Murphy (1996) and Schön (1983).

Chapter 1

1 'A conceptual framework explains, either graphically or in narrative form, the main dimensions to be studied—the key factors or variables—and the presumed relationships among them.' (Miles & Huberman, 1984: 28)
2 See the methodologies used by Hunt (1987), Russell et al. (1988) and Munby and Russell (1988) on the development and use of metaphors in education for further detail.
3 The analogies listed are amongst the more popular and revealing ones identified by practitioners in a series of workplace research projects in education and training (the method used is detailed in Scott, 1990).
4 I am indebted to David Hunt (1987) from the Ontario Institute for Studies in Education for this concept.
5 Contingency theory simply says be prepared to use different strategies and tactics in different situations (Fullan, 1982: 99). It acknowledges that there can be no one fixed approach to change that will work across all settings (Sivage et al., 1982: 101–2) and

that there is no one formula but rather that there are 'configurations of variables that, if manipulated, can be successful in one family of settings and not another' (Huberman & Miles, 1984: 34).

6 The Price Waterhouse Change Management Team (1996) have identified 800 books on managing change published in the US alone from 1989 to 1994.

7 See Binney and Williams (1995) for a more detailed discussion.

8 Moses (1995: 13–14) identifies two theories, commonly applied in other contexts which may be of relevance. They are:

  a Maslow's (1954) theory of a hierarchy of needs. The idea here is that the willingness of an educator to become involved in change is determined by whether or not lower order needs like job security, well paid employment, a feeling of being part of a group, being appreciated and so on are first met.

  b Herzberg's 'two factor theory'. Herzberg, Mausner and Snydman (1959) postulate that one set of factors are negative motivators or 'dissatisfiers'—being blocked, going unrewarded, not having one's talents recognised and so on. The other set of factors are positive motivators or 'satisfiers'. These include a sense of achievement, recognition, challenging work, autonomy, opportunities for growth, status and a sense of belonging.

9 This definition is derived from that used by McDonald and Bishop (1990: 12).

10 See Berman and McLaughlin (1977).

11 This notion is summed up nicely in the words of Octavio Paz: 'Wisdom lies in neither fixity nor in change but in the dialectic between the two.'

Chapter 2

1 Fullan (1986: 7) cites the work of Joyce and Showers on 'inservice as coaching'. Their approach consists of teachers learning about the underlying principles of the innovatory practice, seeing it demonstrated by the coach, practising it and obtaining immediate and ongoing feedback and support by a coach.

2 This definition is very similar to that used by McDonald and Bishop (1990: 12).

3 Gonczi (1994) and Ryan (1997) canvass many of the key issues in the current assessment debate.

4 This classification is derived from the original work of Charters and Jones (1973). Others have subsequently taken a similar approach, coming up with their own classification. For example, in the context of training, Kirkpatrick (1975) identified four different domains for

evaluation: (i) reaction (satisfaction levels); (ii) learning (knowledge, skill and attitude acquisition); (iii) behaviour (has learning transferred to job performance); and (iv) results (wider impact on organisational performance).

5 The most recent use of the framework has been with a flexible learning innovation in higher education (Scott, 1996c).

6 This material comes from the research of Ball (1987), Fisher and Ury (1984), Gronn (1983), Hargreaves (1981), Hoyle (1986), Walford (1987), Scott (1990).

7 An excellent follow-up booklet on a comprehensive approach to evaluation planning in post-secondary education is that written by McDonald and Bishop (1990).

Chapter 3

1 Fullan (1982, 1991) makes this distinction and suggests that a bureaucratic norm is still common in many educational organisations.

2 'Groupthink' (Janis, 1972) is the uncritical acceptance and/or suppression of dissent in going along with group decisions (Fullan, 1993: 82). Cox (1995: 62) refers to 'closed groups' whose survival depends on the maintenance of power and who, therefore, have difficulty dealing with change.

3 Balkanisation (the tendency for strong loyalties to form within a group with a consequent indifference or even hostility to other groups) and micropolitics in educational organisations are discussed in some detail by Ball (1987) and Fullan (1993: 82–3). Balkanisation involves the tendency for departments, centres or groups of staff to vie with each other to win resources and to ignore the broader purpose of working together to deliver the best service and programs possible. Many of the micropolitical strategies listed in this book are dedicated to balkanisation and need to be identified, labelled and discouraged.

4 This is a term invented by Andy Hargreaves of the Ontario Institute for Studies in Education to describe the tendency to hold meetings and claim that these are a genuine opportunity to involve staff or clients in the change process when they are not. It describes the tendency for some managers to talk about team work when, in reality, they make all the decisions.

5 The University of Technology, Sydney has recently introduced a collegial form of professional development and review. The system is described in a users' handbook and in a video tape. Both are available from Associate Professor Geoff Scott, UTS, PO Box 123, Broadway NSW 2007, Australia.

6 In Ontario, Canada some 30 000 teachers are reported to be linked by computer in an Electronic Village Project. The network is used by practitioners to get advice from fellow teachers on how best to handle current classroom problems.
7 See Ambrose (1989) and Senge (1990).
8 Handy (1995), Binney and Williams (1995), Farson (1996), Price Waterhouse (1996) and Stacey (1996) all opt for this notion of managing through paradox.

Chapter 4

1 See Oja and Smulyan (1989) for specific references for the people cited throughout this short history. See Chein, Cook and Harding (1948) for details of Lewin's original conception of action research.
2 Winter (1989), however, notes that Lewin still maintained somewhat of a separation between himself as researcher and action in daily practice.
3 Spiralling diagrams like this were first made popular in the 1980s. See for instance the work of Stephen Kemmis (1985). Other useful overviews of similar processes are in Ebbutt (1985) and Burgess (1985)·.
4 As noted already, contingency theory simply says be prepared to use different strategies and tactics in different situations (Fullan, 1982: 99). This contrasts with the 'one best way methods that still characterise most planning thought' (Bryson and Fladmore-Lindquist in Sivage et al., 1982: 101–2). As Miles and Huberman (1984: 34) conclude, 'there is no one formula, rather there are configurations of the variables that, if manipulated, can be successful in one family of settings and not another'.
5 Bell (1984) covers Sources, Records and References (ch. 9), Designing Questionnaires (ch. 10), Conducting and Analysing Interviews (ch. 11), Keeping a Research Diary (ch. 12), Observing and Recording Meetings (ch. 13).
6 These guidelines are built upon those proposed by Elliot (1991: 75).
7 These principles include: ensuring all viewpoints are listened to, not pressuring people to participate against their will, ensuring that those involved emerge feeling that the benefits of participation outweighed the costs, that any sensitive information given is not made public without permission. For further discussion see Scott (1990) and Elliot (1991: 75).
8 The learning contract method is discussed in Scott (1995a) and in Anderson et al. (1996).
9 A dilemma requires a choice (often under considerable time pressure)

between two or more potentially appropriate courses of action which set up a tension which must be resolved one way or the other (Huberman & Miles, 1984: 78).

10 This framework is adapted from Elliot (1991: 88).

11 This is the Education Resources Information Centre in the US. ERIC covers both hard copy (EJ) materials (like journal articles) and materials which are on microfiche (ERIC Document, or ED material). ED materials may not be widely available but it is possible to get copies of the microfiche and run off hard copy from these. ERIC resources are now being digitised.

12 Currently there are about twelve electronic journals on education accessible through the Internet.

13 Data bases which provide full text journals include, ABI Inform, Periodical Abstracts Research and Expanded Academic Index a.s.a.p.

Chapter 5

1 See Fullan (1991) for data on school-based managers, Scott (1997) for a review of data on effective change managers in post-secondary education, Schön (1983, 1987) and Gonczi et al. (1990) for a more general profile of competent professionals, Morgan (1988: 168–9), Binney and Williams (1995) and Farson (1996) for research on leadership in non-educational settings and Tennant (1991) for a review of research on the distinguishing attributes of experts. The attributes identified also align with what 200 practising educators in the author's post-graduate classes on change management over the past decade have highlighted as distinguishing the most effective change leaders they had encountered.

2 This would include making the 'ground rules' for staff involvement clear, quickly acknowledging the receipt of contributions, being able to delegate clearly, effectively and appropriately, being able to gauge the strengths and weaknesses of particular staff, being able to run effective meetings, and mentor effectively.

3 'Contexts' would include the ability to give and receive constructive criticism, to participate effectively in informal communication situations, to avoid management by rumour, to ensure that staff are well informed about key issues, and to engage in principled negotiation.

4 See the outline of micropolitical strategies discussed in Chapter 2 when informal evaluation was discussed.

5 This would include giving realistic praise to staff, publicly supporting them, getting out of the office and onto the 'turf' of staff, giving undivided attention to staff when meeting with them, winning the

confidence and support of administrative staff, and setting up a conducive physical environment at work.

6 See Scott (1997) for a general review; specific sources are as follows. For research on worker and professional competence see Gonczi et al. (1990), NBEET (1990: 42ff), Mansfield (1989: 34), Marsick (1988), Masters and McCurry (1990: 12), Schön (1983, 1987). For research on expertise in a wide range of occupations see the review by Tennant (1991). For specific areas see Ceci and Liker (1986—race-track handicapping), Chase and Simon (1993—chess), Schmidt et al. (1990—medicine), Lawrence (1988—law), Scribner (1986—dairy process workers). For research on teaching competence see Boud (1985), Hunt (1987), Scott (1990, 1991a, 1995a), Chappell (1995), Joyce and Clift (1984), Fullan and Connelly (1987).

7 This research was undertaken as part of a leadership development project at the University of Technology, Sydney. In the project some twelve current and former deans from faculties ranging from business and design, architecture and building to nursing and science were interviewed. The results were used to focus the individual development programs of new deans on the key capabilities necessary to perform effectively in the role.

8 Some writers (for example, Vecchio et al., 1995: 339 and Handy, 1995: 107) have noted that the most effective leaders are able to adopt a range of leadership styles depending on their reading of the situation.

9 For instance, in 1994 Australia's National Board for Education, Employment and Training commissioned the so-called 'Candy Report' to investigate how best to incorporate lifelong learning skills into the undergraduate curriculum of Australian universities. In 1995 this brief was extended to determine how this might best be achieved in schools, TAFE colleges and other forms of post-secondary education.

10 There are numerous examples of how these might operate in post-secondary and higher education. For example, the University of Technology, Sydney's mentoring scheme for academics provides staff with a trained senior academic as a mentor and provides explicit links to a series of electronic learning networks for staff in core development areas like flexible learning and work-based learning.

11 See, for example, the *Finn Report* (AEC, 1991) on post-compulsory education in Australia and the *Candy Report* (NBEET, 1994) on lifelong learning skills and higher education.

Chapter 6

1 Hypotheticals were first made popular on television by Geoffrey Robertson in the mid-1980s (Robertson, 1986). The approach taken in the adult literacy hypothetical is a variation on that adopted by Robertson.
2 Summer Hill Films, Level 2, 136 Chalmers St, Surry Hills NSW 2010, Australia. Phone: (+61 2) 9698 5544. Email: info@shf.com.au

Conclusion

1 In this context 'values' are the personal guidelines which individuals use to make choices about which way to behave in a given situation, about what sorts of changes are to be deemed progressive and about which are seen to be regressive. Values are therefore, in this perspective, closely aligned to morals and ethics.

REFERENCES

Ambrose, P. 1989 *Organisational Learning*, Jossey Bass, San Francisco

Anderson, G., Boud, D. and Sampson, J. 1996 *Learning Contracts: A practical guide*, Kogan Page, London

Association for Supervision and Curriculum Development (ASCD) 1990 *Changing School Culture through Staff Development*, Yearbook of the Association for Supervision and Curriculum Development, Virginia

Australian Education Council 1991 *Young People's Participation in Post-compulsory Education and Training (the Finn Report)*, AGPS, Canberra

Ball, C. 1987 'Towards an enterprise culture', paper given at OECD seminar, 30 June, Sydney Teachers' College

Ball, S. 1987 *The Micropolitics of the School*, Methuen, London

Barraclough and co. 1994 *Management Competencies in Australian Business*, commissioned research, Australian Government Industry Task Force, Canberra

Bell, J. (ed.) 1984 *Conducting Small Scale Investigations in Educational Management*, Chapman, London

Berman, P. and McLaughlin, M.W. 1977 *Federal Programs Supporting Educational Change, Vol III: Implementing and sustaining innovations*, The Rand Corporation, Santa Monica

Binney, G. and Williams, C. 1995 *Leaning into the Future: Changing the way people change organisations*, Brearley, London

Boud, D. (ed.) 1985 *Reflection: Turning experience into learning*, Kogan Page, London

Boud, D. and Feletti, G. (eds) 1991 *The Challenge of Problem-based Learning*, Kogan Page, London

Bullock, A. 1985 *The Humanist Tradition in the West*, Thames & Hudson, London

Burgess, R. (ed.) 1985 *Issues in Educational Research: Qualitative methods*, Falmer Press, Lewes

Bush, R.N. and Bock, J.C. 1982 *Institutionalisation of Educational Change: Case studies of teacher corps' influence on schools of education*, Final Report, ERIC document no. ED 212 573, Office of Educational Research & Improvement, Washington

Candy, P., Creber, G. and O'Leary, J. 1994 *Developing Lifelong Learners through Undergraduate Education*, Commissioned Report No. 28, August, AGPS, Canberra

Ceci, S. and Liker, J. 1986 'Academic and non-academic intelligence: an experimental separation' in R. Sternberg and R. Wagner (eds) *Practical Intelligence*, Cambridge University Press, Cambridge

Chappell, C. 1995 *A High Quality Teaching Workforce in TAFE*, UTS, Sydney

Charters Jnr, W. and Jones, J. 1973 *On Neglect of the Independent Variable in Program Evaluation*, Project MITT Occasional Paper, University of Oregon, Oregon

Chase, W. and Simon, H. 1993 'Perception in chess', *Cognitive Psychology*, 4: 55–81

Chein, I., Cook, S. and Harding, J. 1948 'The field of action research', *American Psychologist*, 3, 43–50

Cooper, R. and Sawaf, A. (eds) 1997 *Executive EQ: Emotional intelligence in business*, Orion, London

Corey, S. 1952 'Action research and the solution of practical problems', *Educational Leadership*, 9, (8): 478–84

Cox, E. 1995 *A Truly Civil Society: 1995 Boyer lectures*, ABC, Sydney

Csikszentmihalyi, M. 1996 *Creativity: Flow and the psychology of discovery and invention*, HarperCollins, New York

Cuttance, P. 1995 'Building high performance school systems', keynote address, *8th International Congress for School Effectiveness and Improvement*, Leeuwarden, the Netherlands, 3–6 Jan

Darkenwald, G. and Merriam, S. 1982 *Adult Education: Foundations of practice*, Harper & Row, New York

Dewey, J. 1930 *The Quest for Certainty*, Allen & Unwin, London

Dewey, J. 1933 *How We Think: A restatement of the relation of reflective thinking to the educative process*, Heath, Massachusetts

Duck, J.D. 1993 'Managing change: the art of balancing', *Harvard Business Review*, Nov–Dec: 110

Ebbutt, D. 1985 'Educational action research' in R. Burgess (ed) *Issues in Educational Research: Qualitative Methods*, Falmer Press, Lewes

Elliot, J. 1991 *Action Research and Educational Change*, Open University Press, Milton Keynes

Elmore, R.F. 1979 'Backward mapping: implementation research and policy decisions', *Political Science Quarterly*, 94, (4): 601–16

Farson, R. 1996 *Management of the Absurd: Paradoxes in leadership*, Simon & Schuster, New York

Feletti, G. 1992 'Learning of competence in medicine: the Newcastle approach', in G. Scott (ed.) *Defining, Developing and Assessing Higher Order Competencies in the Professions*, AVE Monograph, UTS, Sydney

Field, L. 1990 *Skilling Australia*, Longman Cheshire, Melbourne

Field, L. and Ford, W. 1995 *Managing Organisational Learning*, Longman, Melbourne

Fisher, R. and Ury, W. 1984 *Getting to Yes,* Hutchinson, London

Foley, G. 1995 *Understanding Adult Education and Training*, Allen & Unwin, Sydney

Fullan, M. 1982 *The Meaning of Educational Change*, OISE, Toronto

——1986 'Change processes and strategies at the local level', *Elementary School Journal*, 85, (3): 391–421

——1990 'Staff development, innovation and institutional development' in ASCD, *Changing School Culture through Staff Development*, Yearbook of the Association for Supervision and Curriculum Development, Virginia

——1991 *The New Meaning of Educational Change*, Teachers College Press, New York

——1993 *Change Forces: Probing the depths of educational reform*, Falmer Press, London

——1997 'Constructive change for complex times' in A. Hargreaves (ed.) *Positive Change for School Success: ASCD 1997 yearbook*, Alexandria, Vermont

Fullan, M. and Connelly, F. 1987 *Teacher Education in Ontario*, Ontario Ministry of Colleges and Universities, Toronto

Fullan, M. and Hargreaves, A. 1991 *What's Worth Fighting For: Working together for your school*, Ontario Public School Teachers' Federation, Toronto

Fullan, M. and Pomfret, A. 1977 'Research on curriculum instruction and implementation', *Review of Educational Research*, 47, (1), Winter: 335–97

Gardner, H. 1991 *The Unschooled Mind: How children think and how schools should teach*, Basic Books, New York

Gonczi, A. 1994 'Competency based assessment in the professions in Australia', *Assessment in Education*, 1, (1): 27–44

Gonczi, A., Hager, P. and Oliver, L. 1990 *Establishing Competency-based Standards in the Professions*, National Office for Overseas Skill Recognition, DEET, research paper no. 1, AGPS, Canberra

——1992 'Competency based approaches to education', in G. Scott, (ed.) *Defining, Developing and Assessing Higher Order Competencies in the professions*, AVE monograph series, UTS, Sydney

Gronn, P. 1983 'Talk as work', *Administrative Science Quarterly*, 28: 1–21

Hammer, M. and Champy, J. 1993 *Reengineering the Corporation*, HarperCollins, New York

Handy, C. 1995 *The Empty Raincoat*, Arrow, London

Hargreaves, A. 1981 'Contrastive rhetoric and extremist talk' in L. Barton and S. Walker (eds) *Schools, Teachers and Teaching*, Falmer Press, Lewes

Herzberg, F., Mausner, B. and Snyderman, B. 1959 *The Motivation to Work*, John Wiley & Sons, New York

Hopkins, D. 1984 'Drift and change in Canadian teacher education', *Higher Education Review*, 16, (2), Spring: 51–60

Hoyle, E. 1986 *The Politics of School Management*, Hodder, London

Huberman, A.M. 1987 'Steps towards an integrated model of research utilization', *Knowledge: Creation, diffusion and utilization*, 8, (4): 586–611

Huberman, A.M. and Miles, M.B. 1984 *Innovation up Close: How school improvement works*, Plenum, New York

Hunt, D.E. 1987 *Beginning with Ourselves: In practice, theory and human affairs*, OISE, Toronto

Janis, I. 1972 *Victims of Groupthink*, Houghton Mifflin, Boston

Joyce, B. 1990 'The self-educating teacher: empowering teachers through research' in ASCD, *Changing School Culture Through Staff Development*, Yearbook of the Association for Supervision and Curriculum Development, Virginia

Joyce, B. and Clift, R. 1984 'The Phoenix agenda: essential reform in teacher education', *Educational Researcher*, 13, (4), April: 5–18

Joyce, B. and Showers, B. 1980 'Improving inservice training: the messages from research', *Educational Leadership*, 37: 379–85

Kemmis, S. 1985 'A point by point guide to action research for teachers', *The Australian Administrator*, 6, (4): 221–4

Kemmis, S. and McTaggart, R. (eds) 1988 *The Action Research Planner*, 3rd edn, Deakin University, Melbourne

Kirkpatrick, D.L. 1975 *Evaluating Training Programs*, American Society for Training and Development Inc., Washington

Kolb, D. 1984 *Experiential Learning,* Prentice Hall, New Jersey

Lawrence, J. 1988 'Expertise on the bench: modelling magistrates' judicial decision-making' cited in M. Tennant 1991 *Expertise as a Dimension of Adult Development: Implications for adult education*, UTS, Sydney

Lewin, K. 1948 *Resolving Social Conflicts*, Harper & Brothers, New York

Little, J. 1982 'Norms of collegiality and experimentation: workplace conditions of school success, *American Educational Research Journal,* 5, (19): 325–40

Lynn, J. and Jay, A. 1984 *The Complete Yes Minister: The diaries of a cabinet minister*, British Broadcasting Corporation, London

McDonald, R. and Bishop, R. 1990 *Guidelines for ETF Project Evaluation*, Sydney, Training and Development Services, Faculty of Adult Education, UTS, Sydney

McLaughlin, M.W. 1976 'Implementation as mutual adaptation: change in classroom organisation', *Teachers' College Record*, 78: 339–51

Macken, J. 1989 *Award Restructuring*, Federation Press, Sydney

Mansfield, B. 1989 'Competence and standards' in J. Burke (ed.) *Competency Based Education and Training*, Falmer Press, London

Marchese, T.J. 1997 'Sustaining quality enhancement in academic and managerial life' in M. Peterson et al. *Planning and Management for a Changing Environment*, Jossey Bass, San Francisco

Marsick, V.J. 1988 'Learning in the workplace: the case for reflectivity and critical reflectivity', *Adult Education Quarterly*, 38, (4), Summer: 187–98

Maslow, A.H. 1954 *Motivation and Personality*, Harper, New York

Masters, G. and McCurry, D. 1990 *Competency-based Learning in the Professions*, National Office for Overseas Skill Recognition, DEET, research paper no. 2, AGPS, Canberra

Miles, M.B. and Huberman, A.M. 1984 *Qualitative Data Analysis: A source book of new methods*, Sage, California

Mintzberg, H. 1994 *The Rise and Fall of Strategic Planning*, Free Press/Macmillan, New York

Morgan, G.M. 1988 *Riding the Waves of Change: Managerial competencies for a turbulent world,* Jossey Bass, San Francisco

Moses, I. 1995 'Tensions and tendencies in the management of quality and autonomy in Australian higher education', *Australian Universities' Review*, 38, (1): 11–15

Munby, H. and Russell, T. 1988 *Metaphor, Reflection and Teachers' Professional Knowledge*, interim report SSHRC Grant no. 410 86 0060, Queens University, Ontario

Murphy, E. 1996 *Leadership IQ: A personal development process based on a scientific study of a new generation of leaders*, Wiley, New York

National Board of Employment, Education and Training 1990 *The Recognition of Vocational Training and Learning*, NBEET, Canberra

——1994 *Developing Lifelong Learners through Undergraduate Education* ('the Candy Report'), NBEET, Canberra

Oja, S.N. and Smulayan, L. 1989 *Collaborative Action Research: A developmental approach*, Falmer Press, Basingstoke

Parlett, M. and Dearden, G. 1977 *Introduction to Illuminative Evaluation: Studies in higher education*, Pacific Soundings Press, California

Pascale, P. 1990 *Managing on the Edge*, Touchstone, New York

Peters, T.J. and Waterman Jnr, R.H. 1984 *In Search of Excellence,* Harper & Row, Sydney

Peterson, M., Dill, D., Mets, L. and associates 1997 *Planning and Management for a Changing Environment: A handbook for redesigning post-secondary institutions*, Jossey Bass, San Francisco

Popham, W.J. 1993 *Educational Evaluation*, 3rd edn, Allyn & Bacon, Boston

Price Waterhouse Change Integration Team 1996 *The Paradox Principles: How high performance companies manage chaos, complexity and contradiction to achieve superior results,* Irwin, Chicago

Putnam, R. 1993 *Making Democracy Work: Civic traditions in modern Italy*, Princeton University Press, New Jersey

Robertson, G. 1986 *Geoffrey Robertson's Hypotheticals: Dramatisation of the moral dilemmas of the 80s*, Angus & Robertson/ABC, Sydney

Robinson, J. et al. 1985 *Learning Partnerships*, OISE, Toronto

Russell, T. et al. 1988 'Learning the professional knowledge of teaching: metaphors, puzzles and the theory–practice relationship', in P.P. Grimmett and G.L. Erickson (eds) *Reflection in Teacher Education*, Pacific Press, Vancouver

Ryan, G. 1997 *Learner Assessment and Program Evaluation in Problem-based Learning*, Australian Problem-based Learning Network, Sydney

Schmidt, H.G., Norman, G.R. and Boshuizen, H.P.A. 1990 'A

cognitive perspective on medical expertise: Theory and implications', *Academic Medicine*, 65, (10): 411–21

Schön, D. 1983 *The Reflective Practitioner*, Basic Books, New York

——1987 *Educating the Reflective Practitioner*, Jossey Bass, San Francisco

Scott, G. 1990 *The Change Process in a Teacher Education Institution*, Ed.D. thesis, University of Toronto, Toronto

——1991a 'How clever are we in the way we train our workers: the great Australian competence caper', *Training and Development in Australia*, 8, (2): 7–12

——1991b 'How do we know research and development projects in Vocational Education and Training are cost-effective?', *Studies in Continuing Education*, 13, (1): 70–83

——1992a *Managing Change in TAFE and Adult Education*, Faculty of Adult Education Monograph Series, UTS, Sydney

——(ed.) 1992b *Defining, Developing and Assessing Higher Order Competencies in the Professions*, AVE Monograph, UTS, Sydney

——1995a *Teaching and Learning in Diabetes Education*, UTS, Royal North Shore and St Vincents Hospitals, Sydney

——1995b *Program Planning for Diabetes Education*, UTS, Royal North Shore and St Vincents Hospitals, Sydney

——1996a *UTS Service to International Students*, UTS, Sydney

——1996b *Continuous Quality Improvement and Innovation in an Australian University*, International Conference on Evaluating Quality in Higher Education, April, Beijing

——1996c 'The effective management and evaluation of flexible learning innovations in higher education', *Innovations in Education and Training International*, 33, (4), November: 154–70

——1997 'Change, competence and education', in G. Ryan *Learner Assessment and Program Evaluation in Problem-based Learning*, Australian Problem-based Learning Network, Sydney

Scott, G., Deer, C., McClung, M., Minton, L., Ramsay, R., Scott, K., Siepin, C., Thomas, A. and Walker, K. 1996 *Evaluation of the Innovative Links Program: UTS Roundtable*,

UTS and National Professional Development Program, Sydney

Scott, G. and Kemmis, R. 1996 *The Role of Dean in a Period of Rapid Change*, commissioned report, Office of the Deputy Vice-Chancellor (Administration), UTS, Sydney

Scott, G. and McDonald, R. 1988 *Focal Points: Alternative approaches to teaching and learning*, slides and booklet, TAFE National R & D Centre, Adelaide

Scott, G. and Wickert, T. 1993 *Competence in Practice*, video tape and booklet, Summerhill Films, Sydney

Scott, G., Wickert, T. and Courtenay, M. 1992 *Breaking New Ground: Challenges for TAFE in the 1999s*, video tape and booklet, UTS and NSW Department of TAFE, Sydney

Scribner, S. 1986 'Thinking in action: some characteristics of practical thought', in R. Sternberg and R. Wagner (eds) *Practical Intelligence*, Cambridge University Press, Cambridge

Senge, P. 1990 *The Fifth Discipline*, Doubleday, New York

Sherrin, N. 1995 *Oxford Dictionary of Humorous Quotations*, Oxford University Press, Oxford

Sivage, C.R. et al. 1982 *Politics, Power and Personality: The roles of deans in Deans' Grant Projects*, ERIC document no. ED 223 588, OSER, Washington

Stacey, R.D. 1996 *Complexity and Creativity in Organisations*, Berrett-Koehler, California

Stenhouse, L. 1978 'Case study and case records: towards a contemporary history of education, *British Educational Research Journal*, 4, (2)

Tennant, M. 1991 'Expertise as a dimension of adult development', *New Education*, 13, (2): 49–56

Tough, A. 1979 *The Adult's Learning Projects: A fresh approach to theory and practice in learning*, 2nd edn, OISE, Toronto

Vecchio, R., Hearn, G. and Southey, G. 1995 *Organisational Behaviour: Life at work in Australia*, Harcourt Brace, Sydney

Video Arts 1990 *The Helping Hand* starring John Cleese, video and booklet, Video Arts, London

Walford, G. 1987 *Restructuring Universities: Politics and power in the management of change*, Croom Helm, London

Wieck, K.E. 1976 'Educational organisations as loosely coupled systems', *Administrative Science Quarterly*, 21: 1–19

Wilson, K.G. and Daviss, B. 1994 *Redesigning Education*, Henry Holt, New York

Winter, R. 1989 *Learning from Experience: Principles and practice in action-research*, Falmer Press, London

Zaltman, G., Duncan, R. and Holbeck, J. 1973 *Innovations and Organisations*, Wiley, New York

INDEX